MUSIC FOR INNER SPACE

for Moses Aaron
mystic, story-teller, friend

MUSIC FOR INNER SPACE

TECHNIQUES FOR MEDITATION
&
VISUALISATION

Nevill Drury

PRISM PRESS, DORSET · SAN LEANDRO, CALIFORNIA
UNITY PRESS · SYDNEY

MUSIC FOR INNER SPACE
Copyright © 1985 by Nevill Drury

First published in the United Kingdom and the U.S.A. by Prism Press,
Bridport, Dorset and P.O. Box 778, San Leandro, California 94577
by arrangement with Bauer Verlag, Freiburg, West Germany.

ISBN 0 907061 74 5

First published in Australia in 1985 by Unity Press,
a division of Nevill & Susan Drury Publishing Pty. Limited,
6a Ortona Road, Lindfield, NSW, 2066, by arrangement with Prism Press, Bridport, Dorset
and Bauer Verlag, Freiburg, West Germany.

National Library of Australia
Cataloguing-in-Publication Data
Drury, Nevill, 1947-
  Music for inner space.
  Bibliography.
  Includes index.
  ISBN 0 9589759 0 6.
  1. Mysticism.   2. Meditation.   3. Magical
  thinking.   I. Title.
  131

Designed by Judy Hungerford
Cover photograph by Robert Berthold
Typeset in Baskerville by Margaret Spooner Typesetting, Dorchester, Dorset.
Printed in England by Purnell & Sons (Book Production) Ltd., Paulton, Bristol.

THE AUTHOR

NEVILL DRURY is an internationally published writer in the field of music and occult mythology. His books include the *Dictionary of Mysticism and the Occult, Vision Quest, Don Juan, Mescalito and Modern Magic, Inner Visions* and *The Shaman and the Magician.* He also has a long-standing interest in experimental styles of synthesiser, and his reviews of inner-space music have appeared regularly in such magazines as *Rolling Stone, Hi-Fi Review, Cosmos* and *Nature & Health.*

Nevill Drury first presented his 'myth and music' workshops at the 1980 International Transpersonal Conference in Melbourne, and his work in this area has developed considerably since then. He now divides his time between writing books, presenting workshops, preparing television documentaries and editing specialist publications. He holds a Masters degree in anthropology and lives in Sydney, Australia.

RELATED TITLES BY THE SAME AUTHOR

The Search for Abraxas (with Stephen Skinner)
The Path of the Chameleon
Frontiers of Consciousness (ed.)
Don Juan, Mescalito and Modern Magic
The Occult Sourcebook (with Gregory Tillett)
Inner Visions
Other Temples, Other Gods (with Gregory Tillett)
The Healing Power
The Shaman and the Magician
Vision Quest
Dictionary of Mysticism and the Occult
Inner Health (ed.)

CONTENTS

PART TWO: MYTH AND COSMOS

ACKNOWLEDGEMENTS

No book is written in total isolation and I am grateful for the advice and encouragement I have received from other writers and occult practitioners over the years. I would especially like to thank Michael Harner for introducing me to the technique of drum-beat meditation and also Jonn Mumford for his valuable comments on Kundalini Yoga.

Other writers whose work has been of considerable value as an indirect influence on my own research include Jean Houston, Robert Masters, Mircea Eliade, Stanislav Grof, John Lilly, Carlos Castaneda and Israel Regardie.

FOREWORD

This book is essentially about music, cosmology and meditation. I am sure there will be some purists who will take exception to some of the blendings of mysticism and music that are suggested here, but I do hope that there are also readers who believe, as I do, that spiritual frameworks which are truly vibrant are themselves capable of transformation. As expressed in the Taoist philosophy of *Yin* and *Yang*, the only thing we can be sure of is that everything changes . . .

I have found in my study of esoteric traditions that beneath the outer veneer of complexity — occult symbols, elusive meanings, passwords and 'keys', and other protective devices — there is a comparatively simple core essence. My sincere aim in this book has been to present that simpler version of each tradition as lucidly as possible and to propose practical exercises involving music and visualisation as an accompaniment.

In world mythology there seems to be a consensus opinion that sound — whether as energy, vibration or the 'Word of God' — gave rise to ideas which in turn created the world. So there is nothing strange in relating music to the techniques of meditation and magical visualisation — indeed, they go hand in hand.

While some readers may be surprised that I am confining my musical sources here to what I call the 'music of inner space' — primarily the contemporary ambient sounds and 'atmospheres' produced by synthesisers — I do not myself believe that is misplaced. After all, we are dealing with altered states of consciousness and in the West the idea of composing music to induce and enhance such states has certainly been an unconventional approach until recently. However, the technology which spawned the synthesiser now allows such a range of rhythms, textures and tonal colours that the potential for producing appropriate meditation music is seemingly unlimited.

The structure of this book calls for some explanation, and it may be that the synthesis I have sought does not become apparent until the later chapters. My approach has been to present background material on several major esoteric traditions alongside an account of trance and meditation music and the various techniques of activating the creative imagination.

The book begins with music, moves through to a discussion of imagery and then presents specific meditation and visualisation exercises which integrate both. Each of the chapters has a 'workshop' section so that theory and practice are combined, and I have endeavoured to present each mystical system in a manner which reduces the intrinsic complexity without destroying vital aspects of belief.

The French Kabbalist Louis Claude de Saint-Martin once said, 'Mystics come from the same country and recognise one another' and I believe this can also be said of the great mystical cosmologies. Beyond the language of specific symbolic frameworks and the bewildering multiplicity of deities it would seem that there is a wonderful energy which sustains the world. That energy can be expressed in music and we can learn to attune ourselves to it.

If we have music within us then we are truly alive.

NEVILL DRURY
Sydney, 1985

PART ONE
SOUND & SYMBOL

CHAPTER ONE

MUSIC & ALTERED STATES OF CONSCIOUSNESS

The power of music to inspire and enchant is universally acknowledged. Who has not seen a rich tapestry of colours in the mind's eye while listening to delicate chamber music, or been swept in the imagination over awesome mountain peaks by the tones of a beautiful flute or pan-pipe?

Music indeed is a type of magic, and is still recognised as such in the simpler, pre-technological societies. Today, in our heavily industrialised western culture it is comparatively more difficult to glimpse the mystical and magical realities which for 'primitive' man co-exist within the pattern of everyday events. From the perspective of modern society, magic is a relic of a former era now outmoded by scientific advances. As technology increasingly defines the realities of contemporary life, and computer print-outs rather than primitive gods determine the proceedings of the day, it is not difficult to understand why much that is loosely termed 'occult' or 'magical' appears obsolete and superstitious.

And yet there is another aspect to consider which has been highlighted by recent developments in modern psychology. The work of Robert Ornstein and other researchers on the two hemispheres of the brain has led many to consider that our society is 'left-hemisphere' dominated: dependent primarily on the functions of logical, orderly thinking and analytical, scientific frameworks, and less drawn to intuitive, non-linear thought which is characteristic of the right-hemisphere.[1]

It may be that the apparently irrational magical traditions offer a chance for modern man to recover a sense of the elusive visionary reality and to explore the archetypal realms of the mind where the sacred images of the gods and goddesses still lie dormant.

Following the rise of the American Transpersonal Movement, which has been influenced by such psychologists as Abraham Maslow, Charles Tart and Stanislav Grof, it has become useful to distinguish between what we may call the 'consensus reality' and altered states of consciousness. The consensus reality is the world we agree upon for practical purposes as the 'real' physical world of everyday events, and our language, communication patterns, cultural values and political structures depend upon it. Altered states of consciousness, on the other hand, are those states of mind which form a spectrum beyond the waking state. They include dreams, trance and dissociation states, reverie, visionary and 'peak' experiences and states of mystical illumination broadly categorised as 'cosmic consciousness'. Until recently such states of mind have not been regarded as 'useful', and there has been a tendency to categorise them in psychological and psychiatric literature as pathological and abnormal. Mystics are classified as escapists — inhabitants of an unreal fantasy world — while shamans are compared to schizophrenics and psychotics.[2]

And yet there are signs that the modern perception of the value of the occult and mystical traditions is changing. As meditation is increasingly accepted in treating and preventing stress-related diseases, and as systematic biofeedback research now confirms the links between the brain-wave states of mystics and yogis and their control of autonomic body functions, it becomes increasingly clear that occult and metaphysical systems offer valuable techniques for expanding the spectrum of human consciousness.[3]

The meditative and mystical use of music is among these techniques. In many primitive cultures music, dance and song are used to induce trance and visionary states of mind and to allow the spirit or soul to journey to the home of the gods or glimpse the magical reality through the 'crack between the worlds'. While the 'transporting' qualities of music are recognised in the West in an intellectual, left-hemisphere sense, specific mind-expansion techniques are a comparatively recent development. There is now increasing interest among psychotherapists and lay practitioners alike in such factors as 'set and setting', belief systems, and the application of music in guided imagery work. For this reason it is useful, and profoundly instructive, to consider the primitive world of trance magic, music and song in order to gain a wider perspective. For it is in the relatively less developed cultures which lack a rational and scientific infra-structure that the intuitive and intangible realities of human consciousness have been grasped.

ALTERED STATES

According to anthropologist Erika Bourguignon, altered states of consciousness seem to occur universally and are 'subject to a great deal of cultural patterning, stylisation, ritualisation and rationalising mythology'.[4] And yet certain patterns are apparent.

Following a five-year cross-cultural study which she completed in 1973, Professor Bourguignon found that in 90 percent of all documented societies altered states occurred within a religious framework. She also found it useful to distinguish between general trance and possession trance states. General trance states were characteristic of North American and South American societies, possession states more typical of African cultures.

In North and South America, trance is invariably associated with some form of 'vision quest', where the shaman contacts a guardian spirit in an altered state of consciousness often induced by fasting or psychedelic drugs. On the other hand, among such African peoples as the Zulu, the Nguni, the Swazi and the Xhosa, possession trance is the common pattern: the possessing spirits are summoned in healing ceremonies and then exorcised by diviners. Both in Africa and in what Bourguignon terms 'West African' cultures — including the Caribbean — possession trance may occur spontaneously or be induced through singing, drumming or dancing, but there is relatively less emphasis on the use of psychedelics.

Both trance and possession trance societies offer useful insights for the development of guided imagery work, as will become apparent in subsequent chapters of this book. There is no doubt, however, that from earliest times music has played a very important role in heightening magical consciousness and linking man, nature and the cosmos.

SONGS OF NATURE

In primitive societies the worlds of nature and supernature co-exist. The universe abounds with spirits — some of them hostile, many of them benevolent — and man's destiny depends as much on the will of the gods and ancestor spirits as it does on the events of climate, seasonal change and environment. Eskimo shamans summon their guardian spirits to control the weather, while African Bushmen address the rain in their ceremonies as if it were an animal which could be chided for behaving improperly. Gabon Pygmies sing songs to appease malicious ghosts whom they believe are responsible for causing elephant stampedes, and also believe that the Moon allows ghosts to go abroad at night. The Semang people of Malaysia, on the other hand, have a cheerful relationship with the supernatural beings whom they call the Chenoi and address a number of songs to them. The Chenoi are happy and friendly, and are considered to be the active power in many living things — not unlike the occult concept of nature-spirits and *devas*. Descending to earth by a rainbow called 'The Sun's Road', the Chenoi clap their hands to bring rain-storms for the fruit crops and flowers.

This Semang song shows a sense of joy and exuberance:

'They rub flowers together in the meadow,
They play in the waterspring,
They are glad to follow one another,
All Chenoi together
All rise up and away,
Wander together,
Loud is their laughter,
They love the scent . . .'[5]

THE RISE OF THE SHAMAN

Especially among hunter-gatherer groups, where the food supply tends to be unpredictable, it has been necessary from earliest times for the tribesfolk to seek divine guidance and have intermediaries who could liaise between the tribe and the gods. It was in this way that the role of the shaman originally arose. Here, through means of a trance state induced by various techniques — whether by the monotonous beating of a drum, hallucinatory sacraments or sensory deprivation — the shaman became known as one who could journey 'in the spirit' from the earth-plane to other realms of existence. The gods would then explain to the shaman exactly how many animals could be slain in the hunt, to ensure that taboos were not being broken, and provide sacred, initiatory knowledge. And in this process, as Western La Barre notes in his major work *The Ghost Dance*, shamans learned to imitate the sounds of animals:

'If the reindeer shaman of the underworld controls the fertility of animals, magic success in the hunt and by derivation wealth and plenty, it is the bird shaman who is associated with the weather and the spirits of the sky. (And) there is another feature inextricably entwined with shamanism — music and magic songs. For to become like animals and birds, one must not only dress in their skins and masks, but also imitate their behaviours. In addition to birds' mastery of the air, which shamans achieve in trance and in their flying dreams, the major attribute of birds is their song . . . '[6]

Accordingly, the Yakut shamans of Siberia learned to imitate the lapwing, falcon, eagle and cuckoo with remarkable facility, while the Kirghiz shamans similarly learned not only bird-songs but how to imitate the sounds of their wings. And it was through these acts of imitation that the shamans identified their tribes with totem animals — which came to represent a source of power and a personal link with nature and cosmos.

The early musical instruments — the drum, rasp, rattle, harp — were invariably regarded as magical because they were used in ceremonies to drive away evil spirits or to communicate with the gods. Among the Yakut and Buryat peoples the shaman's drum was called the 'shaman's horse', which is hardly surprising because the monotonous rhythm which emanated from it was suggestive of a galloping horse and the shaman 'rode' his drum-beat into the other world. Similarly the Kirghiz shamans used a magical stringed instrument called a *kobuz* to accompany the dance which induced a trance state.

MUSIC AND TRANCE

Quite apart from the magical significance of the instruments, certain forms of musical expression are ideal for facilitating trance states. Rhythmic drumming or percussion accompanied by vigorous dancing and hand-clapping, for example, is powerful and evocative and stimulates dancers to lose themselves in a flurry of sounds. Such dancing might also cause exhaustion or a change in breathing patterns, leading to hyperventilation — both of which in turn produce a sense of dissociation. Dancing in circles — which also occurs in modern witchcraft and among Sufi dervishes — likewise changes one's sense of equilibrium and can lead to dizziness: another form of altered state.

In this context music and dance go side by side. A sense of excitement builds up as the musicians beat upon their drums, shake their rattles and conjure an atmosphere of expectation. Meanwhile the dancer increasingly surrenders to the persuasive rhythms of the music, becomes intoxicated by it, and enters a state of trance.

Such a situation is to be expected because music and creative expression are closely related. It is through movement and gesture that the essence of music is experienced and, in purely physiological terms, as musicologists Manfred Clynes and Janice Walker point out, 'the central nervous system and the neuromuscular system transform a musical rhythm into a movement pattern'. As they also note, very appropriately, 'the rhythmic experience of sound largely is not under control — we are *driven* by it . . .'[7]

It is not surprising, then, that the characteristic rhythms which induce trance states are repetitive, energetic and often loud and overwhelming. They lead the dancer away from the familiar setting of the everyday world into a disorienting atmosphere pulsing with vibrant rhythms, which usually builds to a climax. In voodoo it is at this point that the *loa* gods possess and 'ride' their subjects in trance like horses, while in Africa the dancers imitate the movements and footsteps of the possessing spirits.

The following account of trance dance describes practitioners of the Macumba spiritist religion in Brazil. Macumba combines Haitian voodoo, African animism and Latin American belief in spirit possession:

'The music was wild tonight, the drums and the licence they were issuing for abandon. Three black men beat at them with a sure sense of their power, and the crowd jammed together heel to toe, clapping along, and gave its amen to the sermon the drums were preaching. The ring of dancers stamped to the beat, but they could only move inch by inch through the throng.

At the centre of their circle, a light-brown boy was bent forward at the waist, shivering a dozen times for every fast clap on the drums. His feet were negotiating the same steps as the other dancers, but he moved so fast he put the rest into slow motion. If I was looking for a mindless joy it was here, in a dance with the brain turned off and the body taking its orders straight from the drums.'[8]

MODERN EXPRESSIONS

While shamanism and Macumba are certainly exotic forms of religious musical expression, the use of drum rhythms to produce altered states of consciousness also occurs closer to home. Prominent among the new mystical sects who have achieved popularity in the United States and Europe are the Krishna Consciousness movement and the *sannyasins* of Bhagwan Shree Rajneesh — both of whom employ music for trance and meditation.

The Krishna Consciousness movement — popularly known as the Hare Krishnas — became known in the West after A.C. Bhaktivedanta Swami Prabhupad brought his particular form of devotional yoga to New York in 1965. Publicly declaring their love for the Hindu god Krishna — himself identified with the flute — sect members began to attract widespread attention by parading in city streets garbed in saffron robes. Chanting 'Hare Krishna' in a mantric chorus and accompanying themselves with brass cymbals, flutes, pipes and drums, they were highly visible and musically intense. In *The New Religious Consciousness*, Gregory Johnson provides an excellent description of a Hare Krishna temple meeting in San Francisco, highlighting the emotional impact of the music:

'The chanting ceremony (mantra) increased in tempo and in volume. Two girls in long saffron robes were now dancing to the chant. The leader of the chant began to cry the words: Hare Krishna, Hare Krishna, Krishna, Krishna,

Hare, Hare; Hare Rama, Hare Rama, Rama, Rama, Hare, Hare. *The entire group repeated the words, and attempted to maintain the leader's intonation and rhythm. Many of the participants played musical instruments. The leader was beating a hand drum in time with his chanting. The two swaying, dancing girls were playing finger cymbals. One young man was blowing a seashell; another was beating on a tambourine . . .*

'The music and the chanting grew very loud and fast. The drum was ceaselessly pounding. Many of the devotees started personal shouts, hands upstretched, amidst the general chant. The leader knelt in front of a picture of the group's "spiritual master" on a small shrine near the front of the room. The chanting culminated in a loud crescendo and the room became silent . . .'[9]

Indian spiritual leader Bhagwan Shree Rajneesh — formerly of Poona and now head of a large meditation community in Oregon — similarly encourages his followers to surrender themselves to their music. Rajneesh advocates meditation as a means of emptying the mind and has developed techniques which produce a state of catharsis. A particular form, Dynamic Meditation, is practised daily for an hour and is accompanied by intense, chaotic music. After a phase of rapid breathing the *sannyasins* plunge themselves into a free-form state:

'Explode! Let go of everything that needs to be thrown out. Go totally mad, scream, shout, cry, jump, shake, dance, sing, laugh, throw yourself around. Hold nothing back, keep your whole body moving . . .'[10]

This is followed by a ten-minute sequence of jumping and shouting, culminating in total exhaustion.

Elsewhere Rajneesh comments specifically on the impact of drumming for meditation:

'Music can become tremendously helpful, but then one has to become completely lost in it. So play the drums and just remember one thing: by and by lose the player completely so that there are only drums and playing, and the player is no more. You will start hearing the drums within yourself. You will be playing outside on the drums and something corresponding to it will start happening within you. Then for the first time you will become the drummer. Then you are in tune . . .'[11]

THE COSMIC SIGNIFICANCE OF SOUND

In many primitive societies and ancient mythologies alike, sound has been regarded as the very basis of existence. Through sound, man and his world came into being and continue to be sustained. Sacred sound — irrespective of its manifestation as music, songs, chants or magical incantations — is perceived in these cosmologies as a vital force or energy which permeates all aspects of creation.

In western religion the concept is familiar enough. In the opening paragraph of *The Book of John* (I.i) it is written:

'In the beginning was the Word, and the Word was with God, and the Word was God. He was in the beginning with God; all things were made through Him, and without Him was not anything made that was made.'

Similarly in *Psalms XXIX iii* we find the reference, *'The voice of the Lord is upon the waters.'*

According to the Kabbalistic *Book of Splendour*, the world came into existence through the utterances of the Sacred Name of God (subsequently condensed into the unpronouncable but nevertheless sacred Tetragrammaton JHVH), and in the Ethiopian Gnostic text *Lefefa Sedek* God is said to have created both Himself and the Universe through the utterance of his own name. For this reason, as Sir Wallis Budge notes in his commentary on the text, 'the Name of God was the Essence of God (and) was not only the source of His power but also the seat of His very Life, and was to all intents and purposes His Soul.'[12]

In ancient Egyptian cosmology the ibis-headed God of Wisdom, Thoth, used words in order to create the universe, calling out over the waters, 'Come unto me . . .', and as we see from reading the Egyptian Books of the Dead, the Sun-god was able to vanquish the powers of darkness by his knowledge of the deities of the Underworld. When the *hekau*, or magical words of power, were uttered the Sun-god gained dominance over the hideous monsters and serpents who lurked in the dark recesses and fiery streams of the Tuat because these utterances or vibrations *were their essence*. Pronouncing their names was thus equivalent to mastering their very being.

Similarly, in Babylonian cosmology the gods mothered by Tiamat in the waters of life, did not emerge as created beings *until they were named*.[13]

In many primitive societies sound and vibration have similar significance. As we have already seen, Siberian shamans use songs to imitate animals and thereby tap sources of magical power, and many primitive tribes use songs to exorcise evil spirits or summon benevolent forces. Sound can also be used in initiation.

Among the Wiradjuri Aborigines, for example, Baiame is the Supreme God — a very old man seated on a crystal throne. He has a long beard and two enormous quartz crystals extend from his shoulders to the sky above. Baiame appears to the Wiradjuri in their dreams and initiates the neophytes by pouring liquid quartz upon them, turning their arms into birds' wings and *singing* quartz into their foreheads. Quartz is considered to possess magical qualities, apparently because it represents 'crystal light' — energy trapped in a solid form — and when Baiame sings the quartz into the neophytes they acquire magical vision and are 'able to see right into things'.[14]

So why does sound play such an important role in mythic and magical belief?

The broad and general answer seems to be that in societies where magic and myth define and influence everyday existence man aspires to be like the gods and to imitate them, thereby acquiring mastery of nature and dominance in the cosmos. In both primitive societies and ancient culture alike, magical incantations and songs are a source of power.

We know from early Gnostic writings that the soul could only earn liberation by knowing the names of the Aeons, or deities of the higher spheres. In ancient Egypt also, the deceased spirit entering the Hall of Judgement asserted before Osiris and the 42 assembled gods, 'No evil will come to me in this land, and in the Hall of the two Maats, *because I know the name of the gods who are of thy company . . .*'[15]

In Kabbalistic magic, in a comparable way, the occultist uses sacred god-names which he intones in ritual as a source of divine strength. Ceremonial magicians still use such god-names as *Jehovah Aloah Va Daath* ('God is manifest as the mind'), *Shaddai El Chai* ('Almighty Living God') and *Adonai Ha Aretz* ('Lord of the Earth') as vibratory incantations to arouse the spiritual energy centres within the body.

Similarly, in primitive society, knowledge of magical sound bestows special powers. Musicologist Marius Schneider summarises the process:

*'To the primitive mind, the phenomenon here called "rhythm" are spirits, the audible souls of the dead ancestors who created all things, and in which they constantly reincarnate themselves. They are the physical and metaphysical reality which is the source of all life and all magical song . . . Anyone who knows and can imitate the specific sound of an object is also in possession of the energy with which the object is charged. The purpose of magic is to utilise this indwelling energy (*orenda, mana, sila, manitu, kami *etc.).'*[16]

Schneider also comments on the ceremonial aspects of music:

'Music for worship consists in a repetition of the act of creation. Admittedly it has not the creative power which enabled the divine ancestors to call forth matter from nothing by their shining songs and war-dances, but its power is analogous and has the power to renew life . . . sound nourishes and preserves both gods and men. In the sky reside sun and moon, lightning and thunder, which give man sunshine and rain. The sounds of earth, human songs of praise, nourish the celestial spirits.'[17]

MUSIC OF THE GODS

In many primitive societies, as we have seen, sound is the direct link between man and the gods. Some Australian Aborigines, for example, believe that their creator gods dwell in bull-roarers which may be whirled in the air to restore energy and vibrancy to both tribe and totem. In shamanic tradition, song is similarly a bridge to the sacred reality and, in its most profound aspects, is summoned from within the shaman's own being. Anthropologist Joan Halifax writes:

'As the World Tree stands at the centre of the vast planes of the cosmos, song stands at the intimate centre of the cosmos of the individual. At that moment when the shaman song emerges, when the sacred breath rises up from the depths of the heart, the centre is found, and the source of all that is divine has been tapped.'[18]

A wonderful description of this process is provided by the North American Gitksan Indian, Isaac Tens. At the age of thirty, Tens began to fall continually into trance states and experienced dramatic, and often terrifying, visions. On one occasion animal spirits and snake-like trees seemed to be chasing him and an owl took hold of him, catching his face and trying to lift him up. Later, while Tens was on a hunting trip, an owl appeared to him again, high up in a cedar tree. Tens shot the owl and went to retrieve it in the bushes, but found to his amazement that it had disappeared. He then hastened back towards his village, puzzled and alarmed, but on the way again fell into a trance:

'When I came to, my head was buried in a snowbank. I got up and walked on the ice up the river to the village. There I met my father who had just come out to look for me, for he had missed me. We went back together to my house. Then my heart started to beat fast, and I began to tremble, just as had happened a while before, when the halaaits *(medicine-men) were trying to fix me up. My flesh seemed to be boiling . . . my body was quivering. While I remained in this state, I began to sing. A chant was coming out of me without my being able to do anything to stop it. Many things appeared to me presently: huge birds and other animals. They were calling me. I saw a* meskyawawderh *(a kind of bird) and a* mesqagweeuk *(bullhead fish). These were visible only to me, not to the others in my house. Such visions happen when a man is about to become a* halaait; *they occur of their own accord. The songs force themselves out complete without any attempt to compose them. But I learned and memorised these songs by repeating them.'*[19]

While such visions may seem to belong solely to the exotic world of the 'primitive imagination' it is interesting that urban westerners who find themselves in a shamanic context sometimes report comparable initiations. The magical apprenticeship of Carlos

Castaneda to the Yaqui sorcerer Don Juan is well known and remains somewhat controversial.[20] However, an equally impressive account is provided by the distinguished American anthropologist Michael J.Harner, now Associate Professor at the New School for Social Research, New York.

In 1959, Harner was invited by the American Museum of Natural History to study the Conibo Indians of the Peruvian Amazon. He set off the following year for the Ucayali River and found the Indians friendly and receptive on his arrival. Harner, however, wished to be more than an anthropologist: he hoped to be initiated as a shaman. He was told that to tap the magical reality he would have to drink the sacred potion *ayahuasca*, made from the Banisteriopsis vine. *Ayahuasca* contains the alkaloids harmine and harmaline and produces out-of-the-body experiences, telepathic and psychic impressions and spectacular visions. Among the Conibo the sacred drink was also known as 'the little death' and its powers were regarded with awe.

Harner took the shamanic potion at night, accompanied by an elder of the village. Soon the sound of a waterfall filled his ears and his body became numb. As he began to hallucinate he became aware of a giant crocodile, from whose jaws rushed a torrent of water. These waters formed an ocean and Harner saw a dragon-headed ship sailing towards him. Several hundred oars propelled the vessel, producing a rhythmic, swishing sound as it moved along. Harner now experienced the music of inner space:

'I became conscious . . . of the most beautiful singing I have ever heard in my life, high-pitched and ethereal, emanating from myriad voices on board the galley. As I looked more closely at the deck, I could make out large numbers of people with the heads of blue jays and the bodies of humans, not unlike the bird-headed gods of ancient Egyptian tomb paintings. At the same time, some energy-essence began to float from my chest up into the boat . . .'[21]

Harner's mind now seemed to function on several levels as he was granted sacred visions by the space-creatures — secrets, they told him, which would normally be given only to those about to die. These visions included a survey of the birth of the earth, aeons before the advent of man, and an explanation of how human consciousness had evolved.

In traditional shamanism, irrespective of its cultural context, it is not uncommon for the shaman to be shown by the gods how society came into existence, how the worlds were formed, and how man and the gods have a privileged and special relationship. What is interesting about Michael Harner's account is that he was able to enter the shaman's exotic world so totally, despite his western intellectual background.

ORPHEUS AND PYTHAGORAS

The figure of Orpheus from ancient Greek legend provides us with an archetypal shaman musician — an enchanter who used his music to summon birds and animals and whose head continued to sing and give oracles long after his death.

According to mythic tradition, Orpheus obtained his lyre from Apollo. When he played his instrument rivers stopped to listen, wild beasts became tame and gentle, and even the mountains moved closer to hear his music. As a mythic figure Orpheus takes his place in Greek legend as the son of Calliope and the husband of Eurydice. When she died from snake-bite Orpheus journeyed to the Under-world, his lyre in his hand, to try to win her back to life. Hades and Persephone — rulers of the nether regions — agreed to allow Eurydice to return to the world of the living provided Orpheus did not look back at her as they ventured home together. Unfortunately, Orpheus turned his head to see if Eurydice was following him, and she was lost to him forever. Orpheus was himself later torn to pieces by the Thracian Bacchantes — the worshippers of Bacchus and Dionysus.

Within the Orpheus legend several interesting themes emerge. Like all shamans, Orpheus has a rapport with nature and his music has magical, transforming qualities. He gives magical prophecies and also visits the Underworld. However, he returns alive — a hallmark of the shaman's vocation as a master of death (the trance-state also simulates death while the shaman's soul goes on its journey).

In ancient Greece the Orphic Mysteries had an importance comparable to those at Eleusis, and members of the Orphic sect held to the doctrine of *soma sema* — 'the body is a tomb'. It was only through the release of the soul to the highest heaven (*Aither*) that true liberation could be attained, and the dismemberment of Orpheus — the destruction of his 'tomb' — characterised this release.

The Bacchantes who had brought about Orpheus' death them-selves used frenzied music and dancing to enter trance states in their religious worship. Wearing long, flowing garments made from fox-skins, and ivy wreaths and horns upon their heads, they brandished daggers and live snakes in their hands and danced to a fever pitch — intoxicated by the spirit of Dionysus. Classics scholar Erwin Rohde summarises the proceedings:

'The ceremony took place on mountain heights at dead of night, by the flickering light of torches. Loud music resounded; the clashing of brazen cymbals, the deep thunder of great hand-tympani and in the intervals the "sounds luring to madness" of the deep-toned flutes whose soul was first awakened by the

Phrygian Auletes. Excited by this wild music the crowd of revellers dances with piercing cries. We hear nothing of any song; the fury of the dance leaves no breath for it. For this is not the measured dance-step with which Homer's Greeks swung rhythmically forward on the Paean, but in a frenzied, whirling and violent round the ecstatic crowd hastens upwards over the mountain-sides.'[22]

Rohde has no doubt that the music and revelry had a powerful effect:

'The terrors of the night, the music, especially of those Phrygian flutes to whose sounds the Greeks attributed the power of rendering the hearer "full of the god", the whirling dance: all these could really create in certain predisposed natures a state of visionary excitement in which the inspired saw as existing independently of themselves all that they thought and imagined . . .'[23]

Of course, the ancient Greek approach to music was not confined to displays of frenzy. The Greek sage Pythagoras (sixth century B.C.) drew strongly on the Orphic tradition in relating music to the sacred, but his concept of the 'harmony of the spheres' was more of an intellectual construct. According to Pythagoras, who compared the structure of harmonious music to mathematical patterns in the cosmos, the distances between the planets formed a ratio like the scales of a musical series. Knowledge of these musical proportions was an important part of the mystery teachings in Pythagoras' school at Krotona, and he believed that numbers and musical notes were like the 'life energies' in the universe — archetypes of creation. However, as Dane Rudyar indicates, for the Greeks of Pythagoras' era cosmic truth was dependent on reason and proportion, and beauty was an aspect of harmonious design. 'What the Greeks meant by harmony in music' says Rudyar, 'is what we call melody . . . and Pythagoras's concepts dealt with a single series of tones.'[24]

So although the concept of the 'harmony of spheres' is both grand and evocative, and has a meditative connotation transplanted into our modern context, it is unlikely that Pythagorean initiates used the monochord series to enter altered states of consciousness.[25] There is no doubt, though, that Pythagoras and members of his school did use music as a healing therapy. They certainly believed that the harmony of sound could restore balance to a diseased person, but their orderly and rational approach contrasts markedly to the spontaneous trance frenzy of the Dionysian worshippers.

MANTRAS

It is in the Indian mystical tradition that we find, for the first time, an elaborate system for using music specifically as an aid to meditative levels of consciousness.

In Yoga and Mahayana Buddhism, sacred intonations or *mantras* are used by devotees specifically to focus the mind and achieve altered states of consciousness. Because both of these spiritual traditions advocate non-attachment to the senses and physical world, sound is used to convey an overriding spiritual reality. As the meditator focuses his mind on one sound alone, repeating it in a cyclic chant, he channels his consciousness in such a way that the wanderings of the mind disappear. Rational restrictions, mental conceptualisation and other impediments of the intellect are transcended as intuition comes to the fore.

The essence of the mantra is monotony — an endlessly repeated sound — and, paradoxically, in Yoga and Buddhism this may lead to enlightenment if employed in the right way. For it is only by vigorously denying the multiplicity of forms in the universe and by transcending the illusion of subject and object, of creator and created, that union with the Godhead occurs. The mantra, as sacred sound, embodies the principle of unity of mind, whether the final aim is union with one's deity (as in Bhakti Yoga) or dissolution in the Void (the Mahayana Buddhist's *sunyata*). The mantra is repeated continually so that the reality of the sound may become all-dominant in the consciousness of the practitioner. As Lama Anagarika Govinda emphasises in his *Foundations of Tibetan Buddhism*, 'Within its sound it calls forth its content into a state of immediate reality: mantra is power.'[26] It is also of interest, as many authorities on Eastern mysticism — including W.Y. Evans-Wentz and Agehananda Bharati — have stressed, that the most powerful mantras of all are those intoned inwardly.

Historically mantras may originally have been incantations to ward off danger, illness and evil spirits.[27] The mantras or *parittas* described in ancient Pali texts were certainly used for this purpose. However, it is in Yoga and Mahayana Buddhism that the mantra reaches its most profound expression.

OM or AUM is the definitive mantra or, as the *Chandogya Upanishad* puts it, 'the best of all essences, the highest — deserving the highest place . . .' For Govinda it is the 'seed-syllable (*bija mantra*) of the Universe, the magic word par excellence . . . the universal force of all-embracing consciousness.'[28] OM represents the beginning, and 'opening', of nearly every mantra, and like the drum of the shaman transports the devotee to the other world of the 'higher reality'.

The *Mundaka Upanishad* compares the mantra to firing an arrow:

'Having taken as a bow the great weapon of the Secret Teaching,
One should fix in it the arrow sharpened by constant Meditation,
Drawing it with a mind filled with That (Brahman),

Penetrate, O good-looking youth, that Imperishable as the Mark,
The pranava *(OM) is the bow; the arrrow is the self;*
Brahman is said to be the mark.
With heedfulness is It to be penetrated;
One should become one with It as the arrow in the mark.'[29]

The same *Upanishad* identifies the sound values of OM (AUM) the following way:

'A' represents the waking consciousness (jagrat)
'U' represents the dream consciousness (svapna) *and*
'M' represents the consciousness during deep sleep (susupti)

We may compare the last of these states to the awakening of cosmic consciousness. Govinda identifies the three stages as:

'A' : ordinary consciousness
'U' : consciousness of the inner world (thoughts, feelings, desires)
'M' : consciousness of the undifferentiated unity.[30]

He also notes that OM taken as a whole represents the 'all-encompassing cosmic consciousness . . . the consciousness of the fourth dimension.' Heinrich Zimmer expresses it somewhat differently, identifying the fourth component as Silence.[31]

The significance of the mantra is reflected in a principle of myth and cosmology mentioned earlier. It is through sound that the world comes into existence and because the creative force is identified with the Godhead, or Supreme Reality, the mystic — in seeking to realise his inner divine self — arouses the sacred rhythms within his own being. In such a way he rediscovers his one-ness with the Universe.

It is for this reason that OM may be described as 'the primordial sound of timeless reality . . . the eternal rhythm of all that moves, a rhythm in which law becomes the expression of perfect freedom.'[32]

DRONES AND RAGAS

Indian musicians have developed specific musical forms to accommodate their mystical disciplines, but the central characteristic of Indian music is the 'drone'. In drone music a central pitch is sustained throughout the composition, and variations of timbre, texture and mood provide it with musical colour and depth. For example, the typical Indian *raga*, which is generally performed with a sitar or sarod accompanied by tablas, has a three-part cycle which develops around a single, sustained note. The introductory *alap* builds the mood and has an improvised, irregular pulse; the *jor* which follows establishes movement through rhythm (without tablas), and the *gat* adds tablas and confirms the cyclic pattern of the composition. Overlaid on the *raga* is the component of melody (*jhala*), which is provided by the virtuoso musician — the sarod or sitar soloist.

Indian *ragas* are thus layers of sound which interweave within themselves, providing a richness of tone and colour to stimulate the imagination. As the *raga* gathers pace in the final phase the mind is able to race ahead, exploring the nuances of mood, enchanted by the meditative spaces between the notes and the images formed in the mind by the escalating rhythms.

It is the drone component — the unchanging basic note or pitch — which sustains the composition and meditatively makes each musical performance an 'inner journey'. One literally travels with the music, lured into new areas of consciousness by the creativity and skill of the musician.

Indian music developed from an understanding of the human voice and traditionally the recitation of the *Vedas* was an important part of religious observances.[33] So it is understandable, both in a psychological and spiritual sense, that drone chanting — like the intoned mantra — is a powerful tool for altering consciousness.

Chants make the recital of holy words mysterious and private. As Professor Robert Erickson says in *Sound Structure and Music*, 'When used in secret and sacred ceremonial songs, the sounds of speech are inseparable from the musical sound as a whole . . . In an oral tradition the sharp division between the categories of speech and music is often blurred, because of the way in which the ceremonial sounds — secret words, meaningless syllables, individual vowels and consonants, echoic and imitative sounds — are built into the music to form one single whole.'[34]

The drone style is also found elsewhere in Asia. In Japan, Buddhists have evolved the ritual *shomyo* chant form and also feature the beautiful shakuhachi flute — both of which are characterised by a sense of what we might call *musical flow*. There is also a considerable respect in Japanese music for the qualities of silence — found between the notes of the bell, cymbal and drum — which offer a pointer to man's inner spiritual nature.

Similarly, Tibetan choral chanting builds around a single note and ritual performance might last for two hours — accompanied only by hand bells, percussion instruments, horns and drums. The purpose of the music, as one observer has expressed it, is to allow the participants to establish 'the deeper, mystic links between the proportions of the cosmos, the human body and the harmonic series . . .'[35]

If one also considers that the chant may include sacred names of

God known only to initiates, the music then takes on an additional dimension — offering private rapport with one's deity. In the act of chanting the singer and his god, for a timeless moment, become one. This brings with it a sense of exultation, freedom and transcendence.

WORKSHOP

MEDITATION ON THE DRUMBEAT

It is very useful to explore the mantric potential of the drum-beat for facilitating an altered state. The technique described here was taught to me in 1980 by anthropologist Dr Michael Harner. Whereas at that time he was inclined to favour a totally consistent drum-beat, I now prefer a slight increase in pace as the drumming proceeds, and also like to vary the drum-beat patterns to provide the feeling that the magical world of inner space is open to all possibilities.

A large flat drum is ideal and the workshop is conducted with one person drumming and the others meditating.

1: INTRODUCTION TO DRUM-BEAT MEDITATION

Meditators: Relax on the floor or in a comfortable chair, in a darkened room. A single candle can be placed in the centre of the room to provide subdued lighting if required.

Breathe deeply, releasing tension from all parts of the body in sequence. An ideal progressive relaxation is to begin with the feet, relaxing them totally, and then imagine a soothing, calming energy working its way progressively through the body — the legs, abdomen, chest, arms and neck. But don't go to sleep! Focus the awareness in the head.

Drummer: Ask the meditator/s to imagine that when you start drumming they will be able to 'ride' the drum-beat into an altered state, rather like riding a horse. As the drumming gathers pace they should visualise a huge, majestic tree which is so enormous that it could be the axis of the world itself — extending high into the heavens and sending its roots deep into the earth.

At the base of this tree — which is in 'Middle Earth' where we all live — is a large doorway, opening into the trunk. Encourage the meditator/s to approach the doorway in their mind's eye and peer inside, without entering.

The drum-beat should be soft at first, with a lilting, enticing quality. If it is too loud it may prove to be a hindrance rather than an aid to meditation. Alter the volume and intensity of the drumming to suit the size of the room. Try to develop harmonics in your drumming, since this adds a sense of mystery to the journey.

Give a sound of four clear drum-beats to announce the conclusion of the meditation and follow it with a rapid-drumming sequence to call the meditators back to everyday reality.

2: TRANCE JOURNEY TO THE MAGICAL WORLD

Meditators: Follow the same procedure as above, but now pass into the tree and visualise that you are journeying down one of the large roots — at an angle of around 45°. Visualise a light at the end of the root-tunnel and travel towards it. Move through the tunnel without paying too much attention to internal details and focus instead on entering the light.

Pass through into the new domain and look around you. What can you see? Is it a scene from Nature: a familiar or unfamiliar landscape?

Now call in your imagination for a magical 'power animal' to assist you, whether with information or as a guide to the new locale. This ally could take the form of an animal, bird or mythical creature (Michael Harner advises against summoning insects, since these tend not to feature in traditional shamanism). Look for a creature that presents itself to you from four different positions and then trust that animal as your own source of inner power.

Go with the creature on your journey and endeavour to memorise as much detail as possible — this can be entered later in your meditation diary. Respond to the drum rhythms and use them as energy to propel you through the imaginal landscape. Don't judge or rationalise anything that appears before you — simply go with the flow.

When you hear the four-fold drum signal, prepare to return and thank your power animal for what has been shown to you. Later you may wish to discuss the journey with the workshop leader and your friends.

Drummer: Because this journey is essentially a sacred quest, begin by defining a magical circle around the participants. I like to shake shaman-rattles at the four quarters, beginning in the east and moving clockwise.

Begin the drumming in a gentle way as before and very gradually intensify the pace. However, occasional sequences of more subdued drumming may be interspersed. Again, ensure that the volume of the drumming is appropriate to the size of the room — you don't have to beat ferociously to be effective!

Close your eyes as you drum and engage in the shamanic process. With practice you will find that the drumming tends to proceed by itself and that you too can undertake a meditative journey with the others. An ideal journey-length is 15 minutes.

At the conclusion of the drumming encourage the participants to write down their experiences and share them in group discussion.

Note: You should emphasise that there are no specific analytical 'meanings' to the images which appear on the shaman journey — the process allows the psyche to reveal itself in a direct way. In due course — perhaps over several journeys — the meaning of the images will become clear to the meditator.

VARIATIONS

The magical drum-beat journey can also be made by passing through the trunk of the tree towards the sky — in which case it becomes rather like a totem-pole, with magical animals or 'deities' appearing on the different branches.

Another variation is to imagine oneself rising up into the sky transported by the wafting smoke of a camp-fire.

CHAPTER TWO

IMAGE & ARCHETYPE

THE MUSICAL IMAGE — AND BEYOND

As we have seen, music has a potent capacity to stir the emotions, captivate or liberate the senses through its moods, and evoke powerful images into consciousness. But from what areas of the mind do these images arise, and what role does the imagination play in the creative process?

The musician lives in a world of images. As psychologist Carl Seashore has noted, the composer shapes his music 'by "hearing it out" in his creative imagination through his "mind's ear" . . . his memory and imagination are rich and strong in power of concrete, faithful and vivid tonal imagery (and) this imagery is so fully at his command that he can build the most complex musical structures and hear and feel all the effects of every detailed element before he has written down a note or sounded it out by voice or instrument'. In addition, says Seashore, the musician 'not only hears the music but often lives it out so realistically in his imagination and memory that he sees and feels a response to the persons, instruments, or total situation in the rendition represented.'[1]

We know from the accounts of several famous composers that a vivid imagination is indispensable to the creation of moving and profound works. For example, Wagner, in his autobiography *My Life*, wrote: 'My whole imagination thrilled with images; long lost forms for which I had sought so eagerly shaped themselves ever more and more clearly into realities that lived again . . .'[2]

Schumann also made a similar point: 'The creative imagination of a musician is something very different, and though a picture, an idea may float before him, he is only then happy in his labour when this idea comes to him clothed in lovely melodies.'[3]

Berlioz, meanwhile, revealed that for him dream and reverie states allowed access to a mysterious world of musical forms: 'Last night I dreamt of music, this morning I recalled it all and fell into one of those supernal ecstasies . . . All the tears of my soul poured forth as I listened to those divinely sonorous smiles that radiate from the angels alone. Believe me ... the being who could write such miracles of transcendent melody would be more than mortal'.[4]

Clearly, in music the interplay of sound and image is of vital importance and hearing and sight, after all, are man's dominant senses. In view of this one would consider the faculty of imagination — the capacity to summon visual images into the field of consciousness — to be central to the scientific study of the mind. And yet a survey of psychological thought and literature shows this not to be the case.

Although the pioneering psychoanalysts Sigmund Freud and Carl Jung were both deeply interested in the imagery of the subconscious mind, as psychology developed it soon moved towards more tangible frameworks of analysis, adopting a predominantly behaviouristic approach. The more subjective areas of human experience — values, intuitions, aesthetic ideals, belief systems, sources of creativity — were neglected to such an extent that in the United States, for example, it was not until 1966 that the first scientific work on fantasy was published.[5]

In the last decade, however, there has been a steady revival of interest in the study of consciousness as well as in the specific fields of imagery and creativity. The revival has spanned many disciplines, including anthropology, comparative religion, psychology and psychiatry, and has been encouraged by such figures as Mircea Eliade, Joseph Campbell, Jerome Singer, James Hillman, David Miller and Silvano Arieti, among many others.

While it is now academically permissible to take an eclectic interest in such diverse cultural forms as mythology, art, music and drama, and the imaginal aspects which underlie them, the broadening of approach has been slow and gradual. It is now more apparent that the scientific insistence on measurement, logic and reductionism — characterised by left hemisphere brain function — is only one aspect of human thought and expression, and the faculties of creative intuition and subjective thought, which arise in the right hemisphere, are equally important. Neurological research clearly indicates that the study of total man must, needs be, look to both polarities of consciousness for a balanced perspective on human potential and creativity.

With this in mind, it is useful to consider Freud's and Jung's researches into imagery and the psychological approaches to the imagination which have developed in more recent times.

FROM DREAM TO ARCHETYPE

Sigmund Freud and Carl Jung were the first psychologists to develop systematic methods for probing the unconscious mind. Their methods and viewpoints, however, in due course became quite divergent.

It is to Freud's great credit that he recognised the inter-relatedness of all mental events, including the repressed and censored memories which are channelled into the unconscious mind. Freud also established that the unconscious included basic human drives such as sexuality and aggression which were sources of enormous psychic energy.

It was through his techniques of dreamwork, encompassing the use of 'free association' that Freud began to probe the symbols of the unconscious. By listening to his patients and allowing them to explore their associated memories in an uncensored way, Freud came to realise how dreams provide a sense of psychic balance, channelling unfulfilled desires into consciousness. In his pioneering work *The Interpretation of Dreams* (1900) he wrote:

'Dreams are not to be likened to the unregulated sounds that rise from a musical instrument struck by the blow of some external force instead of a player's hand; they are not meaningless, they are not absurd; they do not imply that one portion of our store of ideas is asleep while another portion is beginning to awake. On the contrary, they are psychical phenomena of complete validity — fulfilment of wishes; they can be inserted into the chain of intelligible waking mental acts; they are constructed by a highly complicated activity of the mind.'[6]

For Freud dreams were primarily connected with wish-fulfilment, and Freud's followers have been inclined to interpret dream symbols in a relatively fixed and predetermined way, correlating particular images with the sex drive or specific neuroses. Dr. Angel Garma's *The Psychoanalysis of Dreams* (1967), for example, identifies specific correlations in dream motifs: for him the symbol of a boat, a canal, a clam, a cone, a purse, a bird's beak, an island, the head and the hand, can all represent the female genitals while symbols as divergent as a knife, a toothbrush, the nose, a carrot, grapes and turnips are associated with the male genitals![7]

Jung soon began to differ from Freud in his approach to dreams. From Jung's viewpoint, to allow a patient to discuss dreams using free association meant moving away from the autonomy of the dream and not allowing it to present its message on its own terms. The ego was bound to get in the way.

Jung felt it was important to acknowledge the spontaneity and directness of a dream as it 'expressed something specific that the unconscious was trying to say'. Whereas Freud tended to uncover sexual motifs in dreams, Jung regarded the individual situation as foremost in solving the language of the dream, rather than attempting to identify motifs like the phallus or vagina. Jung wrote:

'A man may dream of inserting a key in a lock, of wielding a heavy stick, or of breaking down a door with a battering ram. Each of these can be regarded as a sexual allegory. But the fact that his unconscious, for its own purposes, has chosen one of these specific images — it may be the key, the stick or the battering ram — is also of major significance. The real task is to understand why the key has been preferred to the stick, or the stick to the ram. And sometimes this might even lead one to discover that it is not the sexual act at all that is represented but some quite different psychological point . . .'[8]

There were also certain motifs within dreams which seemed to Jung not to belong to the individual psyche at all, and it was the study of these symbols which led him to formulate the concept of the 'collective unconscious'. 'There are many symbols,' he wrote, 'that are not individual but collective in their nature and origin. These are chiefly religious images; their origin is so far buried in the mystery of the past that they seem to have no human source. But they are, in fact, 'collective representations' emanating from primeval dreams and creative fantasies. As such, these images are involuntary spontaneous manifestations and by no means intentional inventions.'[9]

What Jung was saying in effect was that at a certain psychic level images common to the whole of mankind were capable of manifesting in dreams. These symbols were an expression of what he called 'the constantly repeated experiences of humanity', that is to say they were derived from observations about Nature — encompassing the sun, stars, sky, changes of season and so on — which had become, as it were, embedded in the psychic patterns of the human species as a whole.

Jung called these primordial images 'archetypes'. He gives the following example of how these forms came into existence:

'One of the commonest and at the same time most impressive experiences is the apparent movement of the sun every day. We certainly cannot discover anything of the kind in the unconscious, so far as the known physical process is concerned. What we do find, on the other hand, is the myth of the sun here in all its countless modifications. It is this myth *and not the physical process that forms the sun archetype.'*[10]

While the solar motif might appear in different pantheons in the form of different sun-gods — for example as Apollo or Helios in Greece, as Ra in Egypt or as Ohrmazd in Persia — the archetype itself seems to lead its own independent life, appearing almost autonomous. Relating the archetype specifically to myth and cosmology, Jung notes: 'The idea of angels, archangels, "principalities and powers" in St. Paul, the archons of the Gnostics, the heavenly hierarchy of Dionysius the Areopagite, all come from the perception of the relative autonomy of the archetypes ... an archetype contains within it a certain type of power or influence and seizes hold of the psyche with a kind of primeval force.'[11]

By tapping the universal images of religion, art and myth, Jung had begun to probe the unconscious mind at a much deeper level than Freud. Rather than regard dream images simply as repressions of the person experiencing them he was now convinced, especially at the archetypal level, that dreams had a life of their own. As a consequence he turned away altogether from the technique of dream interpretation — which he felt allowed the conscious ego to inflict its attitudes on the dream contents — to an approach he called 'active imagination'. The new method, he believed, would allow the dream its own sense of individual authority.

ACTIVE IMAGINATION AND INDIVIDUATION

Jung's method was to encourage his patients to interact with their dream imagery by consciously 're-entering' the dream through the imagination, rather than interpreting or analysing it. Unlike Freud, who maintained a dialogue with his patient during therapy, Jung believed that active imagination should be conducted by oneself, alone. In a letter to one of his clients Jung describes the method:

'... start with any image, for instance, just with that yellow mass in your dream. Contemplate it and carefully observe how the picture begins to unfold or to change. Don't try to make it into something, just do nothing but observe what its spontaneous changes are. Any mental picture you contemplate in this way will sooner or later change through a spontaneous association that causes a slight alteration of the picture. You must carefully avoid impatient jumping from one subject to another. Hold fast to the one image you have chosen and wait until it changes by itself. Note all these changes and eventually step into the picture yourself, and if it is a speaking figure at all then say what you have to say to that figure and listen to what he or she has to say. Thus you can analyse your unconscious but also give your unconscious a chance to analyse yourself, and therewith you gradually create the unity of conscious and unconscious without which there is no individuation at all.'[12]

Barbara Hannah, an analyst who worked for many years with Jung in Zurich, amplifies this description in her recent work Encounters with the Soul:

'The first thing is to be alone, and as free as possible from being disturbed. Then *one must sit down and concentrate on seeing or hearing whatever comes up from the unconscious. When this is accomplished, and often it is far from easy, the image must be prevented from sinking back down again into the unconscious, by drawing, painting, or writing down whatever has been seen or heard. Sometimes it is possible to express it best by movement or dancing. Some people cannot get in touch with the unconscious directly. An indirect approach that often reveals the unconscious particularly well, is to write stories, apparently about other people. Such stories invariably reveal the parts of the storyteller's own psyche of which he or she is completely unconscious.* '[13]

Hannah also reinforces the point made in Jung's letter that one should 'hold fast to the one image you have chosen' in order to extract its meaning:

'. . . images must not be allowed to change like a kaleidoscope. If the first image is of a bird, for instance, left to itself it may turn with lightning rapidity into a lion, a ship on the sea, a scene from a battle, or whatnot. The technique consists of keeping one's attention on the first image and not letting the bird escape until it has explained why it appeared to us, what message it brings us from the unconscious . . .' [14]

As we can see from these descriptions, Jung's approach was to allow the dream to speak for itself. The patient, meanwhile, in acknowledging that the dream had a life of its own, could focus on, or hold dialogue with, specific dream images in order to grasp their meaning. From Jung's point of view this process facilitated psychological and spiritual growth because the image represented unrecognised facets of the self that could now be incorporated into consciousness.

For Jung, dream symbols thus pointed inwards to a deeper and more profound perception of one's being. As Mary Watkins has noted in her impressive book *Waking Dreams*, the symbol can never be grasped in terms of what we already know. The very nature of it is to take us beyond . . .' By extension, the technique of interacting with one's dream symbols in active imagination enables the individual 'to take responsibility for himself by providing him with a means of coming to terms with his own unconscious material.'[15]

Jung regarded the image as the language of the psyche, the very mirror of the soul. And further, it was the *only* way of glimpsing reality. In *Psychological Types* Jung wrote, 'Every psychic process is an image and an imaging . . . the psyche creates reality every day'.[16] In another work, *Civilisation in Transition*, he emphasised our dependence on images for our perception: 'Psychic existence is the only category of existence of which we have immediate knowledge, since nothing can be known unless it first appears as a psychic image . . .'[17]

As a consequence, although dreams, fantasy and myth seem intangible, in the final analysis there is nothing more real than the image, and nothing more profound than the archetype.

Jung used the term 'individuation' — meaning to make oneself whole — to describe the process of integrating the contents of the unconscious mind. Through active imagination the image could be used to form a bond between conscious and unconscious, leading gradually towards self-realisation. The process included coming to grips with the 'dark' or repressed aspects of the psyche (which Jung called 'the shadow'), amalgamating the inner sexual polarities (the *anima* in man, the *animus* in woman) and making the 'heroic journey' in search of the Holy Grail within. Individuation was thus the surrender of the ego (one's apparent identity) to the self (one's true being). And as Dr. John Battista points out in his essay 'Images of Individuation', the encounter with the self is essentially a mystical experience:

'Imagery of the self is always characterised by a numinous, transcendent quality. Dreams and fantasies of this phase of the individuation process generally are highly organised and present a theme or story. The person is commonly cast in some mythic garb or engaged upon some mythic task. In the course of this adventure the person may well confront other mythic characters — the king, queen, knight, fair maidens, dragons and other beasts. The self, the goal of the quest or journey, is commonly represented by Christ, a ring of power or some mandala figure . . . the individual must submit to the self to be contained by it, and thus transformed.'[18]

Through his work with archetypes and active imagination Jung became the first psychologist to describe the mythology of the soul in terms of the images of consciousness. His approach has subsequently stimulated several schools of thought in the fields of psychotherapy and comparative mythology, and has also provided a basis for the techniques of guided imagery which are the main subject of this book.

In the United States, in particular, the Jungian perspective has given rise to a new framework of analysis which provides important insights in its own right: the archetypal psychology of James Hillman and David Miller.

MANY GODS OR ONE GOD?

A former Director of Studies at the C.G. Jung Institute in Zurich, James Hillman is now the leading advocate of what might well be called 'mythic psychology'. The author of several somewhat complex works, including *The Dream and the Underworld, The Myth of Analysis* and *Re-visioning Psychology*, Hillman has argued consistently for a re-evaluation of modern psychological frameworks. For Hillman, as for Jung, the soul — or psyche — is the appropriate starting point in psychology. In *The Myth of Analysis*, for example, Hillman says: 'Man ... was created in the divine image; the psyche of man somehow mirrors or clings to the divine. So, our psychological descriptions are also in some way descriptions of the divine . . . If man is created in God's image, psychology as a positive, secular science is quite out of the question.'[19]

However, unlike Jung, whose orientation was influenced by Christianity and for whom Christ was a symbol of the self, Hillman believes it is now appropriate to summon the ancient gods and goddesses of ancient Greece as prototypes for the new mythic psychology. For Hillman a return to a polytheistic psychology is necessary if we are to cater for the rich diversity of human experience. Hillman advocates 'an inner Greece of the mind' because the Greek pantheon of gods offers a rich range of sacred images and 'a chance to revision our souls by means of imaginal places and persons . . . We return to Greece in order to rediscover the archetypes of our mind and of our culture.'[20] In Hillman's framework the gods are metaphors for the many facets of human existence and are the 'prime movers' behind our attitudes: 'A polytheistic religion (mythology) must be therefore the first principle of any psychology concerned with the well-being of the soul'.[21]

Hillman's solution is to summon such gods and goddesses as Apollo, Aphrodite, Eros, Dionysus, Hades, Persephone and Pan, among many others, to provide sacred prototypes for human life. In fact it is not so much a case of summoning as acknowledging, for the gods are with us already: 'The psyche is . . . forced by the gods to evolve an archetypal psychology to meet its needs, a psychology based not on the "human" but within the "divine".'[22]

David Miller, Professor of Religion at Syracuse University, endorses the same viewpoint. For him the values we call truth, beauty, justice, peace, love, goodness and pleasure were personified — or made specific — in ancient Greek religion: 'The Gods and Goddesses are the names of the plural patterns of our existence . . . their stories are the paradigms and symbols that allow us to account for, to express, and to celebrate those multiple aspects of reality that otherwise would seem fragmented.'[23]

In his succinct and far-reaching book *The New Polytheism* Miller gives examples of how the Greek gods reflect human endeavour. He identifies Heracles with hard physical work; Ares with war-mongering; Pan, Aphrodite and Eros with love and sensuality; Zeus with administrative power and Apollo with personal control, as examples of god-realities that are still vitally relevant in our own world.

Like Hillman, Miller rejects the barrenness of monotheistic thought — the concept of a Supreme One-ness which is remote from life — and believes that we should once again recognise a multiple divinity. 'All the Gods are within' says Miller, 'and within may mean within the psyche, within the body, within the collective unconscious . . . our task is to incarnate the Gods . . .'[24]

As we will see later, this is identical with magical and shamanic philosophy but seems all the more dramatic within the context of contemporary psychology. Miller has no doubt of the effectiveness of reviving polytheism: 'The psychological advantage of naming the unconscious structures of behaviour and feeling by the names of divinities is that this strategy accurately identifies the nature of the dynamics of the psyche.'[25]

For Hillman the mythic quest has an additional challenge: it involves entering the Underworld and thereby making the transition from the physical world to the domain of Soul or Psyche. In Greek mythology Hades was 'God of Depths, the God of Invisibles' and through his other name, Pluto (meaning 'riches') revealed the wealth within — the potential fullness of vision within each human being. Like Jung, Hillman recognises the autonomous domain of the dream-world which seems almost like another dimension of existence. But for him it is more real than the physical world. 'We are shadows of our souls,' says Hillman, '. . . the underworld of the psyche is a world where there are only psychic images. From the Hades perspective *we are our images*'.[26] Knowledge of Hades is therefore knowledge of self, of purpose, for 'Hades is the "final cause" of every soul'. Indeed, in the same way that the shaman is a master of death — one who can transcend the barriers between the worlds — Hillman finds in death the gateway to greater knowledge. Hades, he says, is the 'unseen reality'.

The great Greek philosopher Heraclitus said much the same thing: 'When we are alive our souls are dead and buried in us, but when we die our souls come to life again, and live'.[27] Not only is this reminiscent of Orpheus, but it also reminds us that consciousness has new frontiers to explore. As Hillman notes: 'The dream-world — the underworld of the unconscious — is a cosmos in its own right, distinct but not completely unrelated to the day world'.[28]

The new mythic psychology therefore calls for us to penetrate these inner domains and encounter the sacred images normally hidden from view. Like shamans, and like Orpheus, we learn to journey to the separate reality — the magical reality — and return to the waking world. We learn to incorporate the mythic within the physical, and be master of both.

GUIDED IMAGERY

The mythic journey to the inner world is not addressed in practical terms within the work of Hillman and Miller, but it does feature strongly in the techniques of those psychotherapists who have used guided imagery techniques to access the unconscious. In this form of therapy the patient is asked to enter imaginal worlds in a systematic way in order to gain greater knowledge of, and control over, unconscious fears, impulses and potentials. The pioneers of this approach include Robert Desoille, Carl Happich and Hanscarl Leuner.

Robert Desouille was a pupil of the distinguished psychotherapist Eugene Caslant and first began to explore guided imagery in the 1930s. Caslant had earlier proposed specific 'symbols of ascent' for use in meditation, including a ladder, staircase and flying chariot. These were based on the principle that to 'ascend' in the imagination seemed to produce a feeling of tranquillity and self-composure. Desoille developed this concept in his notion of the 'directed daydream', in which he encouraged his patients to encounter archetypal symbols through guided imagery. In doing this, Desoille would lead his subjects into such locations as a cave or ocean, or have them encounter mythical beasts — the embodiment of their fears. At the same time he would monitor his patients' entry into each scene and modify its psychological impact by either having them 'descend' into the imagery or climb above it. Like Caslant, Desoille associated the 'upward' meditative direction with positive imagery, feelings of lightness and euphoria, while to travel 'downwards' in the imagination could produce feelings of anxiety and fear associated with the perception of darkness.

For Desoille the guided imagery technique could help the patient overcome personal limitations. His approach can be summarised as follows:

'The patient must learn to control the "archetypes" within himself, to be free from them, and thereby lose his fear of them ... The goal of the technique is to direct the patient toward the fulfilment of his human potentialities through the creative development of man's basic biological impulses into a higher and harmonic idea.'[29]

For Desoille the state of religious awareness aroused in this process was the highest level of mental functioning.

Carl Happich published several writings on guided imagery in Germany in the 1930s and emphasised that the most effective point of departure into the creative imagination lay mid-way on the spectrum between consciousness and unconsciousness. Happich used the term 'symbolic consciousness' to describe this state of active reverie and made use of specific meditative symbols to produce a positive mental effect. These included a) a meadow, b) a mountain, c) a chapel, and d) a bubbling fountain.

Happich used the meadow-image to gauge the mental health of his patients; the balanced and happy person would invariably populate the meadow with children, flowers, or images of Spring. The unhappy or depressed person was more likely to visualise dying vegetation or barrenness, and conjure other negative motifs to fill the landscape.

The mountain, on the other hand, was used as a symbol of aspiration, enabling the meditator to travel imaginally towards an important goal. On the way he had to pass through a forest — symbolising the dark side of his nature — or overcome other obstacles on the journey.

For Happich the chapel image, which followed next in sequence, was a symbol of the religious attitude — the sacred centre of being. Finally, meditating on the bubbly fountain attuned the patient to the energy source of life itself.

Happich was opposed to the use of symbols like a snake or scorpion which could stimulate dangerous or negative emotions and preferred to choose motifs which he felt sure had a positive and transforming effect.

Hanscarl Leuner developed the guided imagery techniques of Carl Happich in the 1950s and similarly advocated the use of 'positive' images. He commenced his therapy sessions with the scenes of the meadow, mountain and brook which, for most people, had an unthreatening connotation. Leuner's system, which he called 'Guided Affective Imagery' included twelve symbolic situations, some of them similar to those proposed by Happich.

a) *A Meadow* Symbolic of Nature and a 'fresh beginning', the meadow was used as the point of entry. The patient first described a meadow that was familiar and was then asked to find another meadow, or part of the present one, that was as yet unknown. Leuner was interested in how much sunlight shone on this imaginary meadow and how long and abundant the grass was that grew there, for he believed these factors to be visual indicators of psychological health.

b) *The Mountain* Leuner regarded the mountain as a symbol of aspiration and gauged the patient's psychological barriers in terms of obstacles that appeared to hinder the ascent. If only small hills appeared in the patient's vision he was then asked to seek high mountains in the distance and climb the highest one available.

c) *The Stream* In psychological terms the image of the stream was used to represent the amount of psychic energy available to the patient, and the depth and width of the stream was taken to be indicative of character, e.g. 'broad-minded', 'shallow'. Obstacles in the stream were symbolic of conflicts in real life.

d) *A House* Leuner considered the house to be an appropriate symbol of the self. The patient might start by visualising a familiar house and then extend it or explore it in an imaginary way. The more imaginary the house, the greater the insights it provided into the makeup of the psyche. The size of each imaginary room in relation to the nature of its contents was indicative of specific personal qualities.

e) *The Ideal Personality* The patient was asked to 'hear' in his imagination the name of a person of the same sex and then visualise that person. Leuner found that the imaginary person often represented the qualities regarded as 'ideal' by the subject.

f) *Animal Symbols* Leuner would ask the subject to visualise the meadow again and then imagine either a cow, a bull or an elephant. The cow was taken to be symbolic of the mother-relationship, the bull or elephant pertinent to the father-relationship. The character-istics of the imagined animal — for example, hostile, friendly, co-operative, loving and so on — were very significant.

g) *Sexual Symbols* Male subjects were asked to visualise a rose — the degree of luxuriance, the richness of colour and the quality of the blossoms (open or still developing) being the significant factors. Female subjects were asked to visualise walking along a road at dusk after an exhausting journey through the countryside. They were then told that an automobile was coming along the road: perhaps they should ask the driver for a lift home? Leuner considered the sex and appearance of the driver as well as the colour and size of the car as especially significant in terms of psycho-sexual development.

h) *A Swampy Pool* Leuner would ask the subject to visualise a swampy pool in the meadow and look down into the waters. Human figures or animals that appeared in the pool, or which rose out of it, were considered to be symbolic of repressed sexuality.

i) *Figure in a Cave* The subject visualised himself waiting in darkness behind a protective tree, watching for a figure to emerge from a cave.

The creature that came forth — perhaps a friend or parent, or even a mythic persona — represented qualities undeveloped in the subject's personality.

j) *An Erupting Volcano* Leuner considered this symbol an ideal gauge of inner tension. The degree of violence and the amount of material erupted were highly indicative of this inner conflict.

k) *A Lion* Leuner asked the subject to visualise a lion and then imagine it confronting someone regarded as an opponent in real life. The reaction of the lion — eating the opponent or lying passively at his or her feet — was indicative of the subject's ability to express himself effectively and interact with competitors.

l) *An Old Picture Book* The subject was asked to imagine a house, explore its cellar and then dig a hole in its earthen floor in order to find an old book buried there. The subject was then asked to describe some of the pictures in the book. Leuner found that his patients often referred to unresolved or unexpressed issues which had arisen in earlier sessions.

Leuner also introduced the notion of the 'inner guide' to his guided imagery work. For him this persona — whether it appeared as an animal or a wise old man — represented the positive directions of the psyche, and the subject was encouraged to communicate with it. There were also several specific strategies for relating to images:

— in a confrontation situation the subject was encouraged to watch the encounter dispassionately rather than struggle to escape

— the subject should ideally seek reconciliation with a hostile image rather than 'wound' or 'kill' it (after all, this counter-attack could rebound on oneself)

— 'magic' fluids or potions could be visualised to relieve pain.

NEW DIRECTIONS WITH GUIDED IMAGERY

There are elements of Leuner's approach in the Silva Mind Control method and in the 'mind games' of Robert Masters and Jean Houston, and there are also parallels between the power animal who leads the shaman into the magical world and Leuner's concept of an inner guide. Indeed, there are many valid approaches to the creative imagination, albeit with different shades of emphasis.

Among contemporary researchers, however, the main issue has been whether imagery-work should be directed or undirected by the session leader and whether one should focus primarily on positive imagery or on 'images of transformation'. From a Jungian perspective the meditator would need to deal with negative imagery as well as positive in order to integrate both polarities of the psyche.

Desoille, Happich and Leuner all made use of a directed mode, leading their subjects into symbolic locations in the imagination according to a pre-determined approach and using specific motifs like the meadow, cave and mountain. Leuner was quite emphatic in stating that the ego should learn to confront the imagination and overcome it, thereby draining the energy of hostile images in the psyche, and although he favoured dialogue with the mind's 'inner guide', its role was essentially passive.

In more recent times, however, there has been a move away from the directed mode to a less controlled situation, and some therapists believe that Jung's emphasis on spontaneous imagery is a more appropriate procedure.

Mary Watkins, who has a Jungian orientation, writes: '. . . the closer the image is to what we know is spontaneously occurring in the imagination, the easier it seems to be to get in touch with the imaginal . . . Thus taking an image or scene from a dream is an excellent way to begin.'[30] Elsewhere she comments, 'There is a harm, I believe, in not being willing to wait for the client to generate his own symbolic situations and modes of being.'[31]

Similarly, philosopher David Levin favours Eastern approaches to consciousness — and in particular Tibetan Tantra — where 'instead of a dynamic unfolding of experience guided by the narrative unfolding, the emphasis is much more on the spontaneous unfolding of the meditator's *own* experiencing process, without any narrative to guide or structure that unfolding after the initial setting has been re-presented'.[32]

Dr. Michael Emmons, a Californian therapist in private practice, favours the concept of the inner guide — incorporating Leuner's approach — but allows it a paramount rather than a minor role. Referring to his imagery work as Inner Source Therapy, Emmons believes that each person contains within himself 'a powerful source of knowledge, a self-contained system of help'. In earlier times this has been variously named 'the deep self', 'the super-conscious', 'the Buddha-nature' and 'the God within', and Emmons believes that it should be allowed 'complete freedom of response' in therapy. While he acknowledges that guided imagery accompanied by biofeedback, music, sensory isolation and even psychedelics can be useful, his own approach is towards what he calls the 'mindfulness-insight' methods of visualisation which are less structured than meditative-concentration methods. In the Inner Source work Emmons uses a non-directive approach with his clients:

To engage in Meditative Therapy one lies down, closes the eyes, and describes visual images, bodily responses *and* thoughts. *The participant and the therapist are to patiently allow the Inner Source to do what it needs to do to help without interruption or interference and without subsequent interpretation. The Inner Source is allowed to begin and end sessions on its own.'*[33]

Other contemporary practitioners, however, continue to favour guided imagery. Dr. David Bresler, for example, who has worked with Dr. Carl Simonton on visualisation treatments for cancer, has recently summarised his viewpoints in an article titled 'Guided Imagery: Healing through the Mind's Eye', co-authored with Dr. Dennis Jaffe. According to Bresler and Jaffe, guided imagery is a method of communicating with autonomic physiological processes which occur outside conscious awareness, including the regulation of breathing, heartbeat and the body's immune system.[34] While their approach is primarily in the use of visualisation for health, rather than to induce encounters with the archetypal images in the psyche, they emphasise that guided imagery can produce profound states of relaxation and that the use of positive mental images is also particularly appropriate in treating the psychosomatic components of disease:

'Imagining a positive future outcome is an important technique for countering the initial negative images, beliefs and expectations a patient may have. In essence it transforms a negative placebo effect into a positive one.'[35]

So, indeed, there are many valuable — and perhaps equally valid — approaches to the imagination. And, interestingly, there is also an extensively developed range of visualisation techniques which derives from a completely different source: the occult tradition of western magic.

OCCULT TECHNIQUES OF VISUALISATION

One of the basic aims of western ceremonial magic is to stimulate the archetypal areas of the imagination. While occult rituals may seem to belong more to the Middle Ages than the 20th century and conjure an impression of haggard witches and sorcerers draped in exotic robes, in reality the occult phenomenon is very much a contemporary affair. Modern American and British witchcraft practices derive substantially from two occultists — Gerald Gardner and Alex Sanders — the second of whom is still alive today. Similarly, most forms of western ceremonial magic derive from such occultists as the French hermeticist Eliphas Levi (1810-75), the Austrian Kabbalist Franz Bardon (d.1958) and magicians associated directly with the Hermetic Order of the Golden Dawn in England. Among the many influential occultists who were members of this magical order in the 1890s were William Butler Yeats, Arthur Edward Waite, MacGregor Mathers and Aleister Crowley. The noted female occultist Dion Fortune and the Anglo-American occult writer Israel Regardie — widely considered the foremost living authority on western magic — were both members of the Stella Matutina, a derivative order of the Golden Dawn established in 1903. Regardie published the complete rituals of the Stella Matutina in four volumes, under the title *The Golden Dawn* (Chicago, 1937-40) and this work remains the key source-book of contemporary occult practice.

Magical ceremonies are performed within a space that has been ritually sanctified. The magical circle is constructed within a room or building designated as the Temple, and members of the group wear ceremonial attire to identify them with mythic deities like Osiris, Horus or Isis (western magic) or incarnate the Horned God or the Great Goddess in her various forms — Astarte, Hecate, Luna, Aphrodite, Diana (witchcraft). Such activities are based on the premise that ceremonial performance has a powerful and evocative impact on the imagination that is capable of, and indeed often does, profoundly alter the perceptions of those taking part.

However, there is another type of magical activity — known by occultists as 'travelling in the spirit vision' — which more directly parallels the psychotherapeutic techniques of guided imagery described earlier.

Remarkable though it may seem, these occult techniques were first described in Golden Dawn order papers which in the main date from 1892-93, seven years prior to the publication of Freud's *The Interpretation of Dreams* and at least two decades before Jung's development of active imagination techniques.[36] The following extracts from these order papers provide a fascinating insight into the magical concept of imagination:

'The uninitiated interpret imagination as something "imaginary" in the popular sense of the word, i.e. something unreal. But imagination is a reality. When a man imagines, he actually creates a form on the astral or even on some higher plane; and this form is as real and objective to intelligent beings on that plane, as our earthly surroundings are to us'
from *Some Thoughts on the Imagination* by Dr. Edward W. Berridge (*Frater Resurgam*), 1983

'Imagination must be distinguished from fancy — from mere roving thoughts, or empty visions. By it we now mean an orderly and intentional mental process and result. Imagination is the creative faculty of the human mind, the plastic energy — the formative power'
additional comments added to the above by Dr. Wynn Westcott (*Frater Non Omnis Moriar*), 1983

The principal aim of the Hermetic Order of the Golden Dawn was to initiate its members through ritual ceremonies associated symbolically with different spheres of the Kabbalistic Tree of Life — a mystical system which will be discussed in a subsequent chapter. The 'spirit vision' techniques, meanwhile, focused primarily on the five symbols of the Elements — Earth, Water, Fire, Air and Spirit — which were used as triggering symbols to induce visionary states of consciousness.

Known as the Tattvas, these symbols were taken from Hindu cosmology and represent one of the few Eastern influences on what was otherwise a Western esoteric tradition. The symbols used in the Golden Dawn are as follows*:

Prithevi   a yellow square: **Earth**
Apas   a silver crescent: **Water**
Tejas   a red equilateral triangle: **Fire**
Vayu   a blue circle: **Air**
Akasha   an indigo or black egg: **Spirit**

It was also possible to combine the Tattvas to make a more subtle sub-division of qualities; in the Golden Dawn it was considered that each of the Elements contained aspects of the others. Certain combination-Tattvas were also correlated with the seven planets of astrology:

Earth of Air	Water of Fire	Earth of Fire	Air of Fire
Saturn	*Jupiter*	*Mars*	*Sol*

Water of Earth	Water of Air	Earth of Water
Venus	*Mercury*	*Luna*

The procedure for using the Tattva symbols was as follows: A card somewhat larger than a standard playing card was made for each of the Tattvas with the symbol painted clearly against a white background. An additional white card was also prepared and a diary kept on hand for recording the visionary impressions. After performing a purification ritual in the room the practitioner sat in a comfortable position facing in the cardinal direction allocated to the Element concerned (East — Air; West — Water; North — Earth). He now fixed his attention upon the Tattva symbol in an alert but receptive manner and maintained his gaze for a reasonable time. Then, with the image firmly implanted in his field of vision he switched his gaze across to the blank white card positioned alongside, allowing the after-image to form against the white background. The occultist then closed his eyes, building the after-image in the mind's eye until it was large enough to become a doorway. Passing through in his imagination, he noted that the 'back' of the door — the side facing towards the inner planes — was

* These symbols differ slightly from the Tattvas used in Kundalini Yoga. See Chapter Four.

identical to the Tattva itself (the reverse of the after-image). It was now possible to explore the imaginal realms associated with the Element before returning through the Tattva door and shrinking it down to its normal size. The procedure concluded with a symbolic 'closing gesture' — for example a clap of the hand — and a further purification ritual. All visionary details were then written in the magical diary.[37]

Inevitably the imaginal locations summoned to view through the Tattvas reflected the nature of the Element concerned. But often the visions themselves included archetypal figures and symbols which seemed to have a life of their own — distinct from the mind of the meditator. Jung later confirmed this phenomenon in his own exploration of psychic images.

The following Tattva visions are from the magical records of Moina Mathers (*Soror Vestigia Nulla Retrorsum*), wife of MacGregor Mathers, co-founder of the Golden Dawn. They form an adjunct to her order paper *Skrying and Astral Projection* (1897) and provide an excellent example of conscious journeys within the mythic imagination:

USING EARTH AND FIRE TATTVAS COMBINED
'. . . the type of land is volcanic. Hill and mountains, hot air, and sunny light. Using a Pentacle, and calling on the Earth Names, I see before me a species of Angelic King Elemental . . . He has a beautiful face, somewhat of the Fire type, yet sweet in expression. He wears a Golden Crown, and a fiery red cloak, opening on a yellow tunic over which being a shirt of mail. In his right hand he bears a wand, the lower end or handle being shaped somewhat as the Pentacle implement, and the staff and upper end being as the Fire Wand. In his left hand (but this I do not clearly see) he bears a Fire Wand; I think that the right hand points upwards and the left downwards, and is a symbol to invoke forces. Little figures of the gnome type come at his call. When commanded, some broke the rocky parts of the Mountain with pick-axes which they carry. Others appear to dig in the ground. In breaking off these rocky pieces, there fall away little bits of bright metal or copper. Some of these Gnomes collected the bits of metal and carried them away in little wallets slung by a baldrick from their shoulders. We followed them and came to some mountainous peaks. From these peaks issued some large and fierce, some hardly perceivable fires. Into cauldrons or bowls placed above these fires, the collected pieces of metal were placed. I was told that this was a lengthy process, but asked that I might see the result of what appeared to be a gradual melting of this metal. I was then shown some bowls containing liquid gold, but not, I imagine, very

pure metal. I again followed my guide, the Angelic King Elemental Ruler, who gave me his name as Atapa, and followed by some Gnomes bearing the bowl of liquid gold, we came, after passing through many subterranean passages out in the mountains, to a huge cavern of immense breadth and height. It was like a Palace cut out of the rock. We passed through rudely cut passages until we reached a large central hall, at the end of which was a dais on which were seated the King and Queen, the courtier Gnomes standing around. This hall seemed lighted by torches, and at intervals were roughly cut pillars. The Gnomes who accompanied us presented to the King and Queen their gold. These latter commanded their attendants to remove this to another apartment. I asked the King and Queen for a further explanation and they, appointing substitutes in their absence, retired to an inner chamber which appeared more elevated than the rest. The architecture here seemed to be of a different kind. This small hall had several sides, each with a door, draped by a curtain. In the centre of the hall was a large tripod receiver containing some of the liquid gold such as that we had brought with us. The King and Queen, who had before worn the colours of Earth now donned, he the red and she the white garments. They then with their Earth-Fire wands invoked and joined their wands over the tripod. There appeared in the air above, a figure such as Atapa, he who had brought me here. He, extending his wand and invoking, caused to appear from each door a figure of a planetary or zodiacal nature. These each in turn held out his wand over the gold, using some sigil which I can but dimly follow. The gold each time appearing to undergo a change. When these last figures have retired again behind the curtains, the King and Queen used a species of ladle and compressed together the gold, making it into solid shapes and placing one of these at each of the curtained doors. Some gold still remained in the bowl. The King and Queen departed, and it seemed to me that I saw a figure again appear from behind each curtain and draw away the pieces of gold.'[38]

USING WATER AND SPIRIT TATTVAS COMBINED
'A wide expanse of water with many reflections of bright light, and occasionally glimpses of rainbow colours appearing. When divine and other names were pronounced, elementals of the mermaid and merman type (would) appear, but few of the other elemental forms. These water forms were extremely changeable, one moment appearing as solid mermaids and mermen, the next melting into foam.

Raising myself by means of the highest symbols I had been taught, and vibrating the names of Water, I rose until the Water vanished, and instead I beheld a mighty world or globe, with its dimensions and divisions of Gods, Angels, elementals and demons — the whole Universe of Water . . . I called on HCOMA and there appeared standing before me a mighty Archangel, with four wings, robed in glistening white and crowned. In one hand, the right, he held a species of trident, and in the left a Cup filled to the brim with an essence which he poured down below on either side . . .'[39]

WORKSHOP

EXPLORING THE IMAGE

1: ACTIVE IMAGINATION

Experiment with Jung's technique of 'active imagination' by taking a distinctive image from a recent dream.

Sit in a comfortable chair, relax and close your eyes. Focus your attention on the dream image and watch the spontaneous changes which flow from it.

Now imagine that you are entering the dream and becoming part of the process.

— What changes do you feel?

— What impressions and thoughts rise into consciousness?

Record the results in a diary.

(Note: resist superficial analysis — the meanings of the dream symbols will become self-evident after a number of sessions)

2: GUIDED AFFECTIVE IMAGERY

Practise with Leuner's images in a group situation. Take turns as 'leader', guiding your fellow meditator/s into an exploration of each of the symbolic locations in turn, over several sessions.

Prepare your own descriptive material to serve as an 'entry' to each of the locations and begin each session with a progressive relaxation (as described in the Workshop for Chapter One). The entries should assist the meditator in visualising each of the locations — the meadow, the mountain, the stream, the house and so on — but should not include descriptions which might pre-empt the conclusion of the meditation. The meditator should be totally spontaneous in completing the imaginal exercise on his/her own. Record the results in a diary.

3: MEDITATION ON THE TATTVAS

Practise the technique described on page 49. First prepare a set of cards with the five Tattva symbols (poster paint or coloured ink on white card is best) and then explore each of the principle Tattvas in individual meditation sessions. These sessions should be at least a week apart.

(Note: the Tattva symbols used in Kundalini Yoga are more authentic than the motifs used in the Golden Dawn, so treat this initial exploration of the images as a practice in visualisation. See Chapter Four)

CHAPTER THREE

MUSIC FOR INNER SPACE

At this stage it may perhaps be helpful to summarise the most important points about mythic and imaginal journeys into the unconscious and the music chosen to accompany these experiences:

— we should remember that techniques of guided imagery and active imagination produce an altered state of consciousness in which, if we probe deeply enough, archetypal symbols will present themselves. Depending on how we relate to these symbols we have the option of either proceeding further into the most sacred and transformative regions of the mind, or withdrawing from the encounter.

— although guided imagery can lead us into symbolic locations it is generally agreed by Jungians and non-Jungians alike that a degree of spontaneity on the inner journey is vitally important. It is, after all, our own inner reality which is of significance, not the framework proposed by the therapist. We must therefore allow ourselves to enter a space in which the psyche can speak to us directly — whether through the symbolism of dreams, visions or archetypal images — and that communication should be *on the psyche's own terms*. Rationalisations, categorisation and frameworks of analysis remove the spontaneous element and invariably fail to capture the essence of the communication.

— music is a powerful means of stimulating unconscious processes, and repetitive rhythms and mantric musical patterns are used universally to induce trance states. However, we have a choice within the altered state of allowing ourselves to surrender to the music and be 'possessed' by its intoxicating rhythms or 'ride' the music or drum-beat on our journey to the inner world. The first of these states, characterised by Erika Bourguignon as possession trance, is essentially similar to mediumism: here the practitioner's will becomes subservient to the possessing spirit or supernatural force summoned in the ritual ceremony, and invariably the dancer or musician who is possessed has no memory of what has occurred during the altered state when regaining consciousness.

The second category of trance is essentially a form of shamanism: here the practitioner's will remains intact, the shaman remains in control of the altered state while establishing a rapport with the gods or sacred images, and also retains memory of the inner journey. The perceptions gained in trance are then put into practice in daily life.

In preparing this book as a guide to the use of music in altered states of consciousness I feel obliged to state here that my preference is for the second method — that of the shaman. This approach is in full accord with the principles of self-actualisation and the development of spiritual growth which are central to transpersonal psychology, the Human Potential movement and most frameworks of contemporary consciousness research. The shaman, by definition, takes responsibility for his visionary journey rather than being dominated by an external power. As the Yaqui magician Don Juan explained to Carlos Castaneda:

'The world is . . . stupendous, awesome, mysterious, unfathomable; my interest has been to convince you that you must assume responsibility for being here, in this marvellous world, in this marvellous desert, in this marvellous time . . . you must learn to make every act count, since you are going to be here only for a short while: in fact, too short for witnessing all the marvels of it.'[1]

In the other situation, however, whether we are possessed by a voodoo *loa* deity or Macumba god, or find our individuality subsumed by the 'spiritual realities' foisted on us by a master or guru, we have surrendered that sense of responsibility for our own actions — thereby allowing the god or master to speak through us as if we were puppets.

This crucial distinction leads us to a subsequent question which is of vital importance: how far can we journey into the psyche with guided imagery and music, and how do we ensure that the images which arise are spontaneous and not simply imposed?

I am well aware that later sections of this book will present material which could be used for passive involvement or simple escapism. However, the aim of the visualisation exercises offered here is to stimulate the sacred images so that they communicate with the meditator in a direct and unimpeded way. As John Lilly has expressed it in his eloquent and important book *Simulations of God*, we should always be prepared to explore the limitations of our beliefs and seek to *transcend* the image, making our inner journeys open-ended. In order to achieve this, says Lilly, 'one's God must be huge, in order to include one's ignorance, the unknown, the ineffable . . . The explorer of inner spaces cannot afford the baggage of fixed beliefs. This baggage is too heavy, too limited and too limiting to allow further exploration'.[2]

Similarly, on guided imagery journeys we should not limit our experiences to the symbolic details presented in the lead-up situation but use them as doorways to spontaneous, and perhaps awesome, encounters with the psyche. The following thoughts about this process are from my earlier book, *Inner Visions*:

'In the contemporary context, the shamanic magician venturing in the astral domains of the Tree (of Life) retains a vigilant alertness while not wishing to limit his symbolic ingress. He may meet illuminating or terrifying magical creatures, he may travel through exciting and exotic landscapes or murky, elastic limbo states, but it is his belief system — the extent to which he ascribes reality to particular symbolic forms — which will contain him. One imagines as an extreme example, the psychic wanderings of a devout fundamentalist Roman Catholic fearful of the negative side of his belief system — the infinite and immensely painful torment of hell flames licking at his flesh. In the sense of John Lilly's explanation he stands trapped by the limitations of his belief. Our same devotee automatically passes through the flame imagery when he ascribes non-reality to it, thus making his belief open-ended.

In the same way we are reminded of the Avam Samoyed shaman who travels in trance to the domain of the cosmic blacksmith, working a bellows over a huge fire in the bowels of the earth. The shaman is 'slain' and boiled over a fire in the cauldron 'for three years'. The blacksmith then forges him a new head, instructs him in mystical powers and reconstitutes his body. The shaman awakes as a revivified being. Considered as a perceptual reality in the fantasy realm of trance, such a shaman would endure intolerable mental agony if he identified with the dismembering process. Seen, however, as a rite of transformation in which the shaman dispassionately observes his own rebirth initiation, the process acquires a quite different significance and magical effect.'[3]

THE QUALITIES OF MUSIC

Music has many therapeutic qualities because of its capacity to stimulate feelings, emotions and associations. Some types of music exude a calming, relaxing quality suitable for alleviating stress, while other forms of music are intense and dramatic and help sharpen the intellect or produce specific, well-formed images in the mind's eye. Some types of music instil a sense of harmony and balance within us, while other discordant forms might leave us restless, on edge, or lacking resolution. Again, music can be trivial and whimsical or profound and inspiring. It can be formal and ponderously structured or very much alive and spontaneous.

Music therapist Mary Priestley has described how she uses such compositions as Mozart's *Clarinet Quintet in A* and *Clarinet Concerto* as relaxation music. In her therapy sessions she encourages her clients to merge with the music, making a mental journey to different parts of the body to ensure that they are 'perfectly relaxed and comfortable'. By contrast, she uses such works as Bartok's *Fifth String Quartet* to arouse feelings of inner violence and power in her client, and then guides that person to release the pent-up tension through visualisation. Similarly Brahm's *First Symphony* is used to stimulate enriching emotions, while she finds the contrapuntal structure of Bach's *Brandenburg Concerto No.4 in G* is ideal for encouraging incisive and analytical thought.[4]

Dr. Stanislav Grof favours calming music at the beginning of his psychotherapy sessions, followed by powerful and evocative music appropriate for the specific purpose at hand. In leading clients towards emotional or spiritual breakthroughs he has found the sacred music of Mozart, Bach, Handel, Berlioz, Verdi, Gounod and Poulenc especially suitable, while relaxing, 'timeless' music by Bach or Vivaldi, or the contemporary composers like Georg Deuter and Steven Halpern is used to bring the session to a close.[5]

What, then, are the qualities in music that produce these responses?

The main psychological qualities of sound are pitch, degree of loudness, time interval and timbre — and we respond to these qualities with sensory capacities which seem to be innate in each of us from birth. What we call the 'tonal' qualities of music are provided by pitch and timbre and manifest as melody and harmony. The dynamism of music, on the other hand, is reflected in loudness, timing, tempo and rhythm.

In creating music the composer blends these ingredients in different degree, employing the contrast of consonance and dissonance to create a variety of tonal images and impressions. As Carl Seashore has noted, 'take out the image from the musical mind and you take out its very essence'.[6]

The music that we will find useful in exploring altered states may take different forms:

— music for relaxation, to allow the meditator to enter the 'waking dream' state of consciousness on the spectrum between normal alertness and sleep

— music to reinforce the specific symbolic associations to be used in guided imagery, e.g. music to suggest a meadow, a mountain, a cave or stream

— music which suggests transformation from one mode to another

— music for encountering the 'dark' or repressed side of the self
— music to 'lift' the consciousness to a transcendental or blissful state

In some situations it is appropriate to use music with strong associational qualities: this form of music literally summons images to mind and therefore has a focusing function. In other situations music with no personal associations may allow a sense of freedom, expansion or release. Such music disperses imagery, breaks down personal limitations and thought barriers, and may bring with it a sense of peace and fulfilment.

Rhythmic music also has special qualities, some of which — as we have seen — are especially useful in inducing an altered state of consciousness. Because it provides alternate periods of sound and silence, the structure inherent in rhythm offers a sense of regularity which stimulates mental perception. However, depending on whether the rhythm is gentle or intense, such music resonates with our whole being and arouses image-association accordingly. Not surprisingly, the rhythmic forms of trance music we have discussed are effective because firstly they engage the meditator's attention and then they allow him to ride with the music into increasingly imaginal realms. In such cases, as we have already noted, a choice finally needs to be made whether to allow the musical rhythms to dominate (or 'possess') the field of consciousness, or be kept subservient to the purpose of consciously exploring the altered state. Irrespective of this choice, it is important to highlight the fact that music opens new worlds to us as the images suggested by association acquire a new life of their own. In a remarkable and magical way, music in an altered state transforms our perception so that imagination becomes reality.

DRUGS AND MYSTICISM: NEW DIRECTIONS IN MODERN MUSIC

In the West, the concept of creating music for altered states of consciousness has only evolved recently and derives substantially from the psychedelic period of the late 1960s. Although in retrospect this era of hippies, hallucinatory drugs and flower-power now seems simplistic, indulgent and perhaps irrelevant, in terms of the development of Western consciousness it was an era of crucial importance. For the first time, large numbers of young people began to explore the contents of the hitherto unconscious mind by bombarding the psyche with psychedelics and dynamic music, by experimenting with new forms of art and dance, and by challenging both conventional Western morality and regimented frameworks of thinking. While the psychedelic period was unquestionably chaotic and undisciplined — as demonstrated by the 'acid happenings' of Ken Kesey's Merry Pranksters and Timothy Leary's antics on the Millbrook estate — it showed many people for the first time that their psychic potential was vast and awesome, that 'reality' extended far beyond the world of physical appearances.[7] The controversial psychedelic gurus Timothy Leary, Ralph Metzner, Baba Ram Dass and Alan Watts, the avant-garde poets like Allen Ginsberg and Lawrence Ferlinghetti, and the visionary novelist Aldous Huxley, became the archetypal leaders of the youth movement, and works like *The Psychedelic Experience, High Priest, The Doors of Perception* and *Heaven and Hell* became the bibles of the counter-culture. The first of Carlos Castaneda's books on psychedelic magical initiation, and John Lilly's *The Centre of the Cyclone* — a description of LSD in a sensory isolation tank — followed soon afterwards.

As frameworks for altered states of consciousness were now desperately required for the inner journey, a new interest developed in the esoteric and spiritual psychologies of both East and West. W.Y. Evans-Wentz's translations of *The Tibetan Book of the Dead*, and *Tibetan Yoga and Secret Doctrines*, Richard Wilhelm's rendition of the *I Ching* and Idris Shah's books on the Sufis became counter-culture bestsellers, as did Hermann Hesse's spiritual novels *Siddharta, Demian, Steppenwolf* and *The Glass-Bead Game*. In the West, the archetypal systems of the Kabbalah, the Tarot and western magic also went through a dramatic revival, and works by A.E. Waite, Aleister Crowley and Eliphas Levi — which may otherwise have faded into obscurity — acquired a new vogue.

Contemporary music of course reflected these interests. The American rock group Steppenwolf, who had borrowed their name from Hesse's novel, included in their repertoire a song called 'Spiritual Fantasy' which described a universal wisdom-tradition. The Welsh folk-singer Donovan, in his melodic song 'Atlantis', meanwhile portrayed the antedeluvian kings as colonisers of the world, recounting how 'All the gods who play in the mythological dramas in all legends, from all lands, came from Atlantis . . .' And David Bowie, in his song 'Quicksand', evoked specific references to the Hermetic Order of the Golden Dawn:

'I'm closer to the Golden Dawn,
Immersed in Crowley's uniform of imagery,
I'm torn between the light and dark,
Where others see their target, divine symmetry . . .'

In the United States, the leading pop group Santana titled their second album *Abraxas*, naming it after the Gnostic god revived by Carl Jung and Hermann Hesse, while in Germany Timothy Leary joined forces with the pioneering electronic rock band Ash Ra Tempel in a concert performance at the Berne Festival on Walpurgis Night, 1972.

Since this time there has been a steady progression of rock albums which draw their inspiration from mythological or occult themes, and which include many such references in their lyrics. The Scottish hippy folk group The Incredible String Band included numerous allusions to classical deities — including Hyperion and Phoebe — on their popular album *Wild Horses*, while English rock-blues singer Graham Bond combined his otherwise ordinary musical compositions with lyrics based on Aleister Crowley's 'magick' and ancient Egyptian mythology. Pete Sinfield — formerly a member of King Crimson — similarly summoned prophets, heroes, pharoahs and a reincarnation theme on the title track of his album *Still*.

This trend still continues to the present day. In 1973 the Berlin-based Ohr record company released the first of several concept albums based on the Tarot: a three-part album featuring Walter Wegmuller, Manuel Gottsching and Klaus Schulze. Other Tarot albums followed the Wegmuller release. Steve Hackett's *Voyage of the Acolyte*, issued in England in 1975, included lyrical allusions to *The High Priestess, The Tower, The Lovers, The Hermit* and *The Hierophant*, while Mike Batt's more recent album, *Tarot Suite* (1979), includes songs based on the symbolism of *The Fool* and the 'Valley of Swords'. Pursuing a similar mystical orientation, the Irish folk-rock group Horslips produced what they described as a 'Celtic Symphony' in 1976. Titled *The Book of Invasions*, it was based on the twelfth century legends of the fairy race, the Tuatha de Danaan, and included such tracks as 'Sword of Light' and 'King of Morning, Queen of Day'. Among other releases reflecting the impact of esoteric thought on rock music are *Yessongs* and *Tales of Topographic Oceans* by Yes, Gong's album *You* — which includes the composition 'Magick Mother Invocation' — and Dave Greenslade's double album *The Pentateuch* (1979), presented in an elaborate format with spectacular fantasy illustrations by Patrick Woodroffe. One should also mention Van Morrison's 1982 release *Beautiful Vision* which acknowledges the direct influence of Theosophist Alice Bailey and her Tibetan 'master' in its lyrics, specifically on the tracks titled 'Dweller on the Threshold' and 'Aryan Mist'.

However, a clear distinction needs to be made between music which draws on occult imagery for its lyrics or general inspiration, and music which may be used to alter one's spectrum of consciousness by virtue of its intrinsic qualities. By this I mean music whose texture, rhythm and harmonies combine to produce an 'environment' conducive to personal growth and self-transformation. Obviously, much of the music which has emerged in the post-psychedelic era, while influenced by the new interest in consciousness, has little to offer on a practical level. And it is the latter category of music — music we can actually use — which is directly relevant to us here as an adjunct to guided imagery and meditation.

Many musicians and composers have helped to develop the genre which I am calling 'music for inner space' and the styles and forms of presentation vary considerably. It is possible, however, to distinguish three broad international styles — in the music which has emerged, respectively, in Britain, Europe and the United States.

BRITAIN

'Cosmic rock' developed in Britain in the late 1960s and early 1970s with the emergence of several new electronic rock groups, including Yes, King Crimson, Hawkwind and The Moody Blues. However, the most distinctive of the new bands was undoubtedly Pink Floyd. After establishing themselves with *A Saucerful of Secrets* Pink Floyd issued the first of several classic albums, *Ummagumma*, in 1969. Recorded live, the double-album included such tracks as 'Astronomy Domine', 'Set the Controls for the Heart of the Sun' and 'Sysyphus', and featured expansive and sustained sequences of synthesiser and piano. Richard Wright's superb work on keyboards and organ was a highlight of the album and, perhaps for the first time in modern rock music, connections were being made — both in the lyrics and in the music — between the images of outer space and the inner worlds of consciousness. After the release in 1970 of *Atom Heart Mother*, characterised by both a sense of musical grandeur and also the special effects so much enjoyed by head-trippers, Pink Floyd went on to produce the album which stands out as one of their masterworks: *Meddle* (1971). Athough the group still allowed lyrics to dominate on the first side of the album, the second side was devoted to an exquisite single composition, 'Echoes'. Largely instrumental, it featured beautiful sequences of vibrato synthesiser, evoking the textures of crystalline space. 'Echoes' concludes with a soaring and uplifting musical effects suggestive of astral projection — implying transformation to another plane of existence.

Although Pink Floyd could undoubtedly have developed the abstract, textural mode established on *Meddle* they chose not to. Their next album, *The Dark Side of the Moon*, brilliant and commercially successful though it was, once again made its impact through its lyrics, rather than through its music, and even included a type of warning:

> 'And if the dam breaks open many years too soon,
> And if there is no room upon the hill,
> And if your hand explores with dark forebodings too,
> I'll see you on the dark side of the moon . . .'

This sense of hesitancy, perhaps even of paranoia, continued with *Wish You Were Here*. In 'Shine On You Crazy Diamond' vocalist Roger Waters' tone was ominous indeed:

> 'Now there's a look in your eyes,
> Like black holes in the sky . . .
> You reached for the moon — threatened
> by shadows at night and exposed in the light . . .'

Such directions in the music of Pink Floyd have since taken an even more dramatic form — in the intense negativity and alienation of *The Wall* and on the recent album *The Final Cut*, which focuses on the hostility and senselessness of the Falklands War.

If Pink Floyd were major pioneers of cosmic rock — and they certainly influenced the important German group Tangerine Dream — they did not develop the pure, simplified style of synthesiser music which later emerged in Europe. For some time British rock music remained complex and diverse, and it was left to other musicians to develop the abstract qualities vital to inner space music.

The rival group King Crimson were a band who, like Pink Floyd, were capable of both richly layered compositions and exquisite simplicity. Their early albums, *In the Court of the Crimson King* and *In the Wake of Poseidon*, were mythic and grand in conception, and it was only on later releases like *Islands* that a simplified range of musical textures began to appear. The sensitivity of King Crimson, in large degree, was due to the creativity of its lead guitarist Robert Fripp who, after the group's fragmentation, went on to record several beautiful works both on his own and with other artists. On *Evening Star* (1975), for example, Fripp teamed with former Roxy Music member Brian Eno to produce one of the most delicate inner space albums ever recorded. Combining electric guitar and synthesiser, *Evening Star* featured the lovely abstract compositions 'Wind on Water', 'Wind on Wind' and 'Evensong'. However, by 1979 Fripp had reverted to a more raucous electronic style and was now paying more attention to lyrics. His solo album *Exposure* had seventeen tracks, only three of them (*Urban Landscape, Water Music I* and *Water Music II*) in the delicate instrumental style of the earlier album.

Fripp's colleague, Brian Eno, on the other hand, has since become Britain's leading exponent of 'minimal' electronic music. Although he has maintained close connections with contemporary rock idioms — as witnessed on his solo albums *Taking Tiger Mountain, Here Come the Warm Jets* and *Before and After Science*, and in his collaboration with Talking Heads — he has also produced some of the finest inner space compositions recorded to date.

In September 1975 Eno evolved a work called 'Discreet Music' by fusing two melody lines while occasionally modifying the timbre of his synthesiser. The effect was a subtle blend of what Eno calls 'gradual processes', resulting in music that was so minimal that it could either be listened to or ignored. Eno was in fact building towards his concept of 'ambience', which he later explained more fully in 1978 with the release of *Ambient One: Music for Airports*. By this stage Eno had become increasingly interested in 'environmental' music — a form he was keen to distinguish from the derivative and watered down mood music used in retail stores and other commercial environments. For Eno the task was to create a series of 'atmospheres' which could evoke a variety of moods. This was quite different from the purpose of 'muzak': 'Whereas the extant canned music companies proceed from the basis of regularising environments by blanketing their acoustic and atmospheric idiosyncrasies, Ambient Music is intended to enhance these. Whereas conventional background music is produced by stripping away all sense of doubt and uncertainty (and thus all genuine interest) from the music, Ambient Music retains these qualities. And whereas their intention is to 'brighten' the environment by adding stimulus to it (thus supposedly alleviating the tedium of routine tasks and levelling out the natural ups and downs of the body rhythms), Ambient Music is intended to induce calm and a space to think.'[8]

Eno also emphasised the somewhat detached quality of his music: 'Ambient Music must be able to accommodate many levels of listening attention without reinforcing one in particular; it must be as ignorable as it is interesting.'

Music for Airports includes beautiful synthesiser and piano sequences and is simultaneously relaxing and engaging. It was followed in 1980 by *Ambient Two: The Plateaux of Mirror*. Here Eno worked with Harold Budd on a series of compositions for piano and synthesiser. The music is at times crystalline, at times reflective, at times diffuse. The mind is free to build images from the sensitive and delicate changes in mood and tone and is lulled from one musical environment to the next. Eno's releases since then have included *Ambient Four: On Land* (1982) and *Apollo* (1983) — music composed to evoke the 'atmosphere' of the successful American space-landing on the moon. *Ambient Four* includes a variety of marsh, wind and beach sound-effects. The music for *Apollo*, on the other hand, captures the awesome mystery of space and the unique adventure of the astronauts. Eno was intrigued by the possibility that Alan Shepard and his colleagues could be experiencing 'a unique mixture of feelings that quite possibly no human had ever experienced before'.[9]

The *Ambient* albums are important works in any catalogue of inner space music and have unquestionably set new standards in recorded synthesiser music. Other relevant works for meditation and imagery work can be found on Eno's *Possible Musics* (co-composed with Jon Hassell), on *Music for Films* (especially the three 'Sparrowfall' tracks), on *The Pearl* and on *Another Green World* ('Becalmed').

Although Eno is now the dominant force in British inner space synthesiser music, he is not alone in his experimentation.

The British rock instrumentalists Jon Field and Tony Duhig, better known as Jade Warrior, recorded a series of albums in the 1970s featuring such musical instruments as harp, gong, glockenspiel, flute, drums, piano, guitar, organ and vibes. Jade Warrior's beautiful first album, *Floating World*, released in 1974, was dedicated to the Japanese philosophy of 'living only for the moment' and 'floating along the river current'. This was followed by *Waves* (1975), which included Steve Winwood on moog and piano, and *Kites* (1976) — an album which opens with musical impressions of a forest. Duhig and Field used tape-recorders to capture the mood of Nature 'as the sun comes up, the forest wakes and the wind begins to blow through the trees'. Subsequent tracks included compositions evoking the sense of floating in the wind, and music to accompany Zen stories attributed to Lu K'uan Yu.

Although the British musicians Steve Hillage, Jon Anderson and Steve Winwood have produced individual compositions of great interest, it is perhaps fair to say that the only other musician to achieve major impact in the inner space genre is Mike Oldfield. Widely recognised for his evocative theme music for the feature film *The Exorcist*, included on the *Tubular Bells* album, Oldfield became known for his remarkable ability to master a wide range of instruments, including guitar, harp, bass, mandolin, bodhran, bazouki and piano. While his earliest recordings, *Tubular Bells* and *Hergist Ridge*, now seem a little dated, Oldfield's music can be exhilarating and powerful, sweeping the listener along with its often intricate melodies. In recent times, as evidenced on his albums *Five Miles Out* and *Crises*, Oldfield has begun to incorporate lyrics into his music — featuring such vocalists as Maggie Reilly and Jon Anderson — and because lyrics in general tend to intrude on a meditative state the latest albums have little interest for guided imagery work. However, several tracks from his middle-phase recordings *Ommadawn* (1975) and *Incantations* (1978) have exciting meditative possibilities.

EUROPE

The development of inner space synthesiser music in Europe is primarily a German phenomenon dominated by Tangerine Dream and Klaus Schulze and other relatively less well known musicians like Yatha Sidhra, Michael Hoenig, Peter Michael Hamel, Cluster, Dzyan and Annexus Quam. However, the Swedish keyboards player Bo Hansson, Greek virtuoso Vangelis and Frenchman Jean Michel Jarre have also made significant contributions. In general terms, while in Britain this form of electronic music has tended to become more simple after complex beginnings, the reverse has been true in Europe. Many of Tangerine Dream's earliest releases were expansive, uncluttered 'space music', while most of the recent albums have tended to promote more distinctive melody lines and heavier rhythms. The work of Jarre, Vangelis and also the Klaus Schulze protege Kitaro is similarly strong on melody while still retaining a fondness for abstract musical textures.

The earliest releases for the Berlin-based group Tangerine Dream remain classics of inner space music. The three-man group — which at that stage comprised Edgar Froese on electric guitar and generator, Chris Franke on synthesiser and cymbals, and Peter Baumann on synthesiser, organ and vibraphone — formed in 1965 and first played conventional rock music in the American style. They listened to the music of Pink Floyd but also to Liszt, Debussy, Wagner, Stockhausen, Ligeti and Sibelius, and were keen to push these musical forms towards a new frontier. Their early albums, *Alpha Centauri* (1971), *Zeit* (1972) and *Atem* (1972-3) retain a sense of romanticism but are very much expressions of space and texture. *Zeit*, for example, opens with cosmic synthesiser and a profound sense of emergence, as expressed in the title of the first track: 'Birth of Liquid Pleiades'. The music evokes the ever-gradual and time-encompassing process of the birth of stars in the universe, and bursts of electric organ seem to herald the possibility of life. On 'Nebulous Dawn' one can imagine light trickling over scarred rock-formations on a forgotten planet while 'Supernatural Probabilities' features unusual voice-like effects suggestive of a strange extra-terrestrial ritual performed by invisible gods.

Tangerine Dream developed this sense of mystery on their later albums *Phaedra* (1974) and *Rubycon* (1975) recorded, like all their subsequent releases, on the English Virgin label. *Phaedra*, named after the doomed daughter of King Minos of Crete, is an album of considerable beauty and dignity. Its second side, which is especially fine, opens with a passage suggestive of *Peer Gynt* and explores silken textures and ethereal forms in an extraordinary, undulating manner as the music seems to unfold from within itself, revealing new moods of expression. *Rubycon* is remarkable for the way in which the double moog synthesiser and organ are able to simulate the effects of inner space voices, capturing a sense of timelessness and awe found elsewhere perhaps only in the works of Ligeti.

As the group began to develop a popular following, Tangerine Dream now began to tour England, playing where possible not in concert halls or auditoriums but in the tranquil and sacred spaces offered by large cathedrals, for example in Coventry and Liverpool. Their audiences sat in total darkness, absorbing the mystery of the music.

Tangerine Dream, however, did not choose to sustain this unified direction in their music, and their next albums, *Ricochet* and *Stratosfear* were less consistent, despite individual compositions of interest. Signs of fragmentation began to appear and by January 1978 — when *Cyclone* was recorded — Peter Baumann had left the group and had been replaced by vocalist Steve Joliffe and percussionist Klaus Krieger. Baumann subsequently recorded two solo albums, *Romance 76* (1976) and *Trans Harmonic Nights* (1979). For the most part his music had less substance than the former work with Froese and Franke and, particularly on the later album, was inclined to be whimsical and melodic — anticipating a change of direction in European synthesiser music as a whole.

Edgar Froese, meanwhile, had recorded two evocative solo albums, *Aqua* (1973-4) and *Epsilon in Malaysian Pale* (1975), the former interesting for its watery effects and mysterious synthesiser sounds, the latter rich and romantic in the style already established by *Phaedra*. But he, too, now inclined towards more pronounced rhythms and melodies with the release of *Ages* in 1978 and *Stuntman* in 1979. Some of the tracks on *Ages*, for example 'Metropolis' and 'Nights of Automatic Women', are urgent and aggressive while 'Icarus' offers a basic three-chord riff similar to Booker T & the MG's rhythm and blues instrumental 'Green Onions'. Simple melody lines dominate on 'Golgotha and the Circle Closes' and 'Ode to Granny A'. Similarly, on *Stuntman*, although 'Scarlet Score for Mescalero' is sumptuous and expansive, the title track offers an electronic melody line simulating Spanish trumpets.

The recent releases of Tangerine Dream are of mixed value for guided imagery work. *Force Majeure* is perhaps their most impressive album in the last five years, featuring unusual percussive effects and lilting synthesiser rhythms. On the other hand, while both *Tangram* (1980) and *Logos* (1981) have the advantage of continuous tracks on both sides, making extended visualisation easier, both albums suffer slightly from rhythmic intrusions that break the mood. *Tangram* is evocative and haunting nevertheless, and *Logos* similarly presents a subtle and reflective quality despite the fact that it was recorded live (at the Dominion, London). *White Eagle* (1982), on the other hand, may prove to be a crossroads for the group. Drawing on the imagery of the American Indian, it offers both gimmicky and whimsical tracks like 'Convention of the 24' and 'White Eagle', as well as more abstract music with a sense of expectancy ('Mojave Plan').

While Tangerine Dream emerged as a powerful musical force in Berlin, another important group had also formed: Ash Ra Tempel. This group did not survive for long as a single entity but two of its members, keyboards player Klaus Schulze and guitarist Manuel Gottsching, have since emerged in their own right as solo performers.

The 1972 release *Join Inn* shows that Ash Ra Tempel had their roots in orthodox rock 'n roll. However, the lengthy instrumental 'Jenseits' on the second side had an exquisite, eerie quality characteristic of early German inner space music. In the same year as *Join Inn*, Schulze released the first of his many solo albums, *Irrlicht*. While it certainly revealed the potential of his late work the album was distant and uncommitted, offering a surprising, and somewhat unsatisfactory blend of church organ monotone and musical textures that sounded like weather effects. *Cyborg*, recorded in 1973 with an elaborate 'Cosmic Orchestra', was more interesting, opening with a carefully layered theme. The second track, 'Conphara', offered rich velvet tones while on 'Chromengel' Schulze interposed his synthesiser with the cello and strings instrumentation of the orchestra, producing a curious high-pitched vibrato. Schulze's best work, however, still lay ahead. *Blackdance* was recorded in 1974 for Metronome and showed the musician's superb facility on synthesiser, organ, piano, percussion and guitar. 'Ways of Changes' merges synthesiser with gentle, acoustic guitar, and there is a sustained rhythm as waves of electronic sound break overhead, like surf over rocks. 'Some Velvet Phasing' shows the muted and dignified side of Schulze's music, while 'Voices of Syn', which makes use of Ernst Walter Siemen's bass chanting, adds a strange pagan quality to the electric organ.

Timewind (1975) produced a new direction altogether: the music was crisp, vibrant and metallic and included unusual humming effects superimposed over steady bass rhythms. At times the textures of the music were misty and rarefied, and at other times rich and deep. 'Bayreuth Return' is especially magical, and although it is dedicated to Wagner it provides more the impression of a shaman's spirit-catcher whirling in the air!

Schulze's next releases, *Moondawn* (1976) and *Mirage* (1977), have similarly established themselves as important inner space albums. 'Floating', the first side of *Moondawn*, features delicate synthesiser sequences and muted rhythm effects while the first half of 'Mindphaser' is ethereal and uplifting. *Mirage*, with its classic composition 'Crystal Lake', remains one of the masterpieces of the genre, and its lilting synthesiser rhythms provide an ideal musical medium for guided imagery.

While the 1977 film soundtrack *Body Love* was less varied than his earlier releases Klaus Schultz produced a fine double album, *X*, in 1979, and has demonstrated with his recent releases *Trancefer* (1981) and *Audentity* (1983) that he is still capable of impressive and imaginative work. Both of these albums have potential application in guided imagery visualisation. *Trancefer* includes sequences where tactile rhythms are incorporated with sounds reminiscent of chanting. 'Silent Running' on the second side, builds from a gentle opening to a well sustained rhythmic tempo, and the tapping effects provide the music with a primitive shamanic quality. And while the double album *Audentity* is at times discordant and hesitant, it too has rich possibilities. 'Armourage' on Side Two begins with echoey, cavernous effects, transforming from subterranean watery impressions to the texture of air, while 'Sebastian im Traum' offers eerie, melancholy impressions similarly suggestive of water and caves. 'Spielglocken' is a type of synthesiser raga whose pace builds gradually, and it too allows a range of musical textures for visualisation. Interestingly, Schulze conceived this work as an expression of the search for self-identity, exploring the impressions and associations provided by his music. As Garry Havrillay writes on the accompanying sleeve notes, 'Voices call from the future and past, doors open and close, dominating his thoughts, reviewing and evaluating . . . There are reflections which menace . . . like insects writhing in the brain, then moments of solitude, some of which are isolated with apprehension and others with serenity'. It is precisely this richness of tonal colour and mood that makes the music useful for guided imagery.

Manuel Gottsching has been less prolific than Klaus Schulze but nevertheless similarly experimental. His individual albums include *Inventions for Electrical Guitar*, recorded in Berlin in 1974, and as Ash Ra, *New Age of Earth* (1976) and *Blackouts* (1977). As a guitarist and synthesiser musician Gottsching inclines towards fully developed rhythmic compositions and as a whole his work lacks Schulze's subtlety. However, specific words like 'Ocean of Tenderness' and 'Quasarsphere' are central to the inner space genre.

Another of Klaus Schulze's proteges also deserves mention: the Japanese synthesiser musician and acoustic guitarist Kitaro. Gentle and graceful, Kitaro's albums are for the most part more mellow than those of Edgar Froese and Klaus Schulze while identifiably part of the same tradition. His albums include *Silk Road I*, *Silk Road II*, *From the Full Moon Story*, *Ten Kai*, *Ki*, *Silver Cloud* and *Oasis*, and the music is ideal to open or close guided imagery sessions. However, Kitaro's development of pronounced melody lines makes the music less suited to visualisation work than the more abstract textural music of his colleagues.

Other German musicians who have produced interesting and experimental work include Michael Hoenig and Peter Michael Hamel. Hoenig was born in Hamburg and studied journalism and theatre at Berlin's Free University. After becoming interested in free-form music in 1968 he began to experiment with electronic sounds and assisted Klaus Schulze in recording *Timewind*. He later toured Australia and England with Tangerine Dream. His solo album *Departure from the Northern Wasteland*, released in 1978, features several fine synthesiser tracks, including 'Hanging Garden Transfer' and 'Voices of Where' — both of which have evocative, abstract qualities. More recently Hoenig has assisted Philip Glass in creating music for the soundtrack of the remarkable film *Koyaanisqatsi*.

Peter Michael Hamel has also had a distinguished musical career and is also the author of the important book *Through Music to the Self*, first published in 1976. After studying composition with Fritz Buechtger and Guenter Bialas at the Music Academy in Munich, he began to compose music for stage, television and opera and has since received several awards for his music, including the Villa Massimo Rome Prize in 1980. A devotee of Indian music, he became strongly involved with meditative styles of composition, especially music featuring a stable pulse and 'modular' structure. Hamel's Indian influence is demonstrated on *The Voice of Silence* and his album with the group Between, *Dharana*, recorded with a symphony orchestra. Another of his albums *Colours of Time*, released in 1980, features meditative synthesiser music based on the cyclic, 'modular' style.

As I mentioned earlier the contemporary European synthesiser musicians these days incline more towards melody than abstract texture. Jean-Michel Jarre achieved international recognition for his albums *Oxygene* and *Equinoxe* and passages from this music have proved suitable for feature films. Similarly Vangelis' *Chariots of Fire* and *Ignacio* were both composed with the requirements of the film medium in mind. Consequently, although this type of electronic music has undoubted evocative qualities it tends to be fragmented and diverse in approach and usually does not extend sufficiently, either in length or mood, to allow a practical application in guided imagery work. It also has the disadvantage, from a meditative viewpoint, of bringing to mind specific image-associations from the film with which it is associated. In the same way, Bo Hansson's electronic albums *Music Inspired by Lord of the Rings* and *Music Inspired by Watership Down* also have limited meditative application because they are related to individual literary works and likewise tend to stimulate specific memory associations rather than archetypal processes in the imagination.

THE UNITED STATES

Contemporary American music encompasses a number of traditions, including the many facets of classical and electronic music, jazz, blues, folk and rock. Not surprisingly the inner space and meditative music which has emerged from the United States has a number of divergent sources. The jazz of John and Alice Coltrane, the guitar music of rock artist Devadip Carlos Santana, the piano of Keith Jarrett and the experimental music of Philip Glass, Steve Reich, La Monte Young and Terry Riley — all of these, at different times and for different listeners, could be said to have meditative qualities. There is also the distinct genre of relaxation music — associated with the work of Steven Halpern and other west-coast musicians — as well as the idiosyncratic blend of the Oregon-based guru Bhagwan Shree Rajneesh. And across the border, Canadian-based New Yorker Paul Horn has produced several beautiful albums of meditative flute music inspired by the Great Pyramid and the Taj Mahal.

Of the new wave musicians, American composer Philip Glass is currently among the most prominent. A winner of Ford Foundation and Fulbright grants for his modular form of music, Glass achieved recognition for his *Music in 12 Parts* (1974) and his operas *Einstein on the Beach* (1976) and *Satyagraha* (1980). He has recently been acclaimed for the remarkable music he has written for the impressionistic film *Koyaanisqatsi* — a uniqe visual sequence of landscapes and urban images. The music itself is often hypnotic and trance-inducing, and features some unforgettable deep chanting.

Terry Riley is also one of the most influential of the new wave musicians and established his 'modal' and 'cyclic' styles prior to the advent of inner space music in Europe. Born in California in 1935, he studied music in San Francisco and went to Europe in 1962, performing as far afield as France and Scandinavia. From a meditative viewpoint, Riley's album *Rainbow in Curved Air*, recorded in 1969, remains his most significant, although *Persian Surgery Dervishes* and *Happy Ending* — released in Europe in the 1970s — earned him an enthusiastic following. In 1980 Riley released *Shri Camel*, a work which had originally been commissioned by Radio Bremen in early 1975. Riley used an elaborate digital delay system to enable him to play duets and trios as an accompaniment to the solo, and to experiment with electronic acoustics. Unfortunately the work suffers from a pronounced heaviness of tone and at times is surprisingly discordant. 'Anthem of the Trinity' seems rather heavy-handed by comparison with the dextrous facility of Klaus Schulze, and 'Celestial Valley' appears to lose direction mid-way. 'Across the Lake of the Ancient Word' and 'Desert of Ice' are perhaps the most successful tracks, showing Riley's virtuosity on keyboards and allowing more spontaneity and freshness in the music.

A far more successful album, from a meditative or 'spiritual' point of view, is Geoffrey Chandler's *Starscapes*, released on the Californian Unity label in 1980. Chandler's music has been accurately described as 'environmental, meditative, transporting and romantic' and at its best can be aptly compared to the most subtle work of Tangerine Dream on *Zeit* and Klaus Schulze on *Moondawn*. Resonant, ethereal and delicate, it is one of the most beautiful inner space albums yet released in the United States.

Other serene and gentle musical works have been issued on cassette (and occasionally on record) by small Californian music companies and are not always easily obtainable. They include music by flautist and zither player Schawkie Roth, the vibraphone and piano compositions of Jon Bernoff and Marcus Allen, the *Golden Voyage* series of Robert Bearns and Ron Dexter and the exquisite *Inner Sanctum* recording of Aeoliah and Larkin. Aeoliah, a German visionary artist and synthesiser musician, combined on this tape with Californian moog-player Don Robertson and the sensitive flautist Larkin, and the result is one of the most beautiful and transcendental inner space compositions yet produced. Larkin has also issued several other fine recordings, including *To the Essence of a Candle, O'cean*, and *Concert Journey*.

71

Allied to this genre is the work of Steven Halpern whose music has been developed specifically for relaxation and self-healing. Halpern did not always play the gentle and sensual music he has become famous for. Originally a trumpeter and guitarist, he gravitated to jazz while studying sociology at the University of Buffalo and was initially influenced by such musicians as saxophonist Archie Shepp and drummer/pianist Joe Chambers. However, Zen and the works of Gurdjieff were fashionable subjects on the campus at the time and Halpern became increasingly interested in mysticism. Some years later, while he was meditating in the woods near Santa Cruz, his perspective in this area deepened. 'I started hearing this gently flowing music', he recalls. 'Basically I heard what became my album *Spectrum Suite* in a couple of seconds.' He walked down the road to a nearby growth centre — 'a kind of mini Esalen' — and began to play on the piano. The music needed developing but the essential ingredients were there. 'Since I had never studied piano,' Halpern says, 'I was working more from sounds that I would hear — phrases and harmonic and melodic combinations.'[10]

Halpern's recent music is delicate and tranquil and tends at times towards blandness. The understated quality, however, is deliberate. Halpern's main aim is to produce music which is therapeutic and he believes that to produce the 'relaxation response' all semblance of a regular beat should be removed. This leaves spaces between the musical phrases and allows the meditative mood to develop — thereby increasing the alpha brain-wave pattern in the consciousness of the listener.

Halpern is a prolific musician and it is not easy to know where to start when presented with a range of his attractively packaged cassettes. Among his best recordings are *Zodiac Suite*, a work combining piano, violin, zither and flutes; *Spectrum Suite*, a solo album which links the seven notes of the musical octave to the seven colours of the visual spectrum, and *Eventide*, which evokes feelings of stillness and peace.

Also offered as meditation music, but often more exuberant and colourful than that, are the diverse musical compositions of the Rajneesh Foundation. Bhagwan noted in his discourse *Music the Ultimate Meditation* that music can create harmony both in our environment and also within each one of us. Accordingly he encouraged the development of meditation music at his former ashram in Poona, and while this music — now marketed from Rajneeshpuram in Oregon — is not as well recorded as its European counterparts, it nevertheless presents a sense of vitality and joy.

The best known of the Rajneesh musicians is German-born

Swami Chaitanya (Georg Deuter), who recorded his early albums at Poona and now lives at Rajneeshpuram. His philosophy of life is a meditative one and consists of 'relating peace, beauty, balance and joy through music'.

Aum was Deuter's first album of meditative music and it included a mix of acoustic instruments, synthesiser and the sounds of the sea. A blend of relaxed moods and rhythmic composition, it is less satisfying than some of his later albums. He followed it with *Celebration*, featuring bells, bird sounds and vibrant guitar strumming, and the beautiful *Ecstasy*, with its evocative flute and guitar. *Haleakala*, inspired by a Hawaiian volcano also known as the House of the Sun, blended vocals with zither, flute, synthesiser and piano, and the often delicate *Silence is the Answer* evoked an Eastern ambience with synthesiser, recorder, guitar and percussion.

While Deuter is undoubtedly the most visible of the Rajneesh Foundation musicians, fellow *sannyasin* Swami Govinddas is also impressive and there are a number of recordings where individual performers are not identified — suggesting that there could be many as yet unrecognised musicians of great talent at Rajneeshpuram. Among the best of the more recent releases are Swami Chaitanya's *Flowers of Silence*, Swami Govinddas' *Just a Glimpse* and the anonymous compositions *Nataraj* and *Nadabrahma*. *Flowers of Silence* features guitar, recorder, shakuhachi, synthesiser and tablas and has some beautiful moments, especially when the recorder comes to the fore. There are also chime effects and classically inspired sequences of acoustic guitar. *Just a Glimpse* similarly offers a diverse range of musical instruments including guitar, mandolin, tambura, sitar and zither, blending western folk music styles with the traditional Indian *raga*. Neither of these is strictly meditational however: *Flowers of Silence* at times evokes a Renaissance atmosphere, and *Just a Glimpse* offers a variety of moods and melodies.

Nataraj and *Nadabrahma*, by contrast, are altogether different. The first of these is written for an exuberant meditation style which divides into three parts. The first, lasting 40 minutes, includes a meditation-dance of total frenzy in which the unconscious mind is encouraged to 'take over completely'. This is followed by 20 minutes of stillness and calm, culminating in five minutes of 'celebration and joy'.

Nadabrahma is composed to accompany an ancient Tibetan meditation technique usually performed either at night or in the early hours of the morning. For the first 30 minutes the practitioner sits relaxed and visualises the body as a hollow vessel. Humming sounds are made in unison with the music. After this the hands are rotated in large outward circles with the palms facing up. Later the palms are faced down and the hands are moved in an inward circular motion toward the body. The meditation ends with a period of silence. The music itself is spacey and cavernous — seeming to flow from the very centre of the earth. Consisting of dark, deep tonal colours, it is for the most part slow and intense, although towards the close it becomes more spirited — as if the soul were freed from its constrictions.

Finally, in summarising some of the main directions of American meditation music mention should be made of Paul Horn's superb flute compositions, Herbie Mann's musical exploration of traditional Japanese art-forms and Henry Wolff and Nancy Hennings' compositions for Tibetan bells.

Horn is best known for his two albums *Inside* and *Inside the Great Pyramid*. The first of these was recorded in 1968 on location in the Taj Mahal — specifically in the central dome which houses the bodies of Shah Jahan and Mumtaz Mahal. Horn found that the dome had remarkable acoustic properties; when an Indian guard called out suddenly the tone and texture of his voice seemed to remain suspended in the air, with voice and echo blending into one. Horn was inspired by the magical atmosphere of the Taj Mahal and recorded several very beautiful compositions there with the permission of the guard — including 'Mantra 1' and 'Vibrations'. Later, in 1976, Horn was invited to visit Egypt with an archaeological team. Several members of the group were interested in examining the Pyramids in terms of 'meditative vibrations', resonances and energy fields. Horn was most impressed by the famous King's Chamber in the Great Pyramid — a majestic room some 34 feet long and 19 feet high, with a ceiling of polished red granite. Awed by the sanctity of the environment, he felt, as he says in his own words, 'a strong spiritual force or energy permeating the atmosphere and simply responded to it'. His recordings there, and also in the Queen's Chamber and in the Kephren Pyramid burial chamber, are masterpieces of meditative flute playing.

American flautist Herbie Mann is usually associated with more mainstream jazz music but he made something of an obscure musical detour in the mid 1970s to explore the textural qualities of Japanese *gagaku* and *shomyo* music. The *gagaku* form of instrumental music dates from the 8th century and has Chinese, Indian and Korean origins. *Shomyo* is a type of Buddhist chant that gained ascendancy in the 11th century and has parallels with the Western Gregorian style. In 1976 Mann took his jazz group to Tokyo and recorded *Gagaku & Beyond*, an impressionistic jazz album that includes a *shomyo* chant, the traditional *shakuhachi* and *koto*, and also the less familiar *sho* mouth organ, *taiko* drum and *samisen* stringed instrument. Because the music derives from a profound spiritual source it has remarkable meditative and guided imagery possibilities and represents, for Mann, 'the expansion of both Eastern and Western ideals'.

Avant-garde musicians Henry Wolff and Nancy Hennings have similarly turned to the East for their mystical expression using only Tibetan bells. Their music is ethereal and timeless, often sounding like electronic inner space music despite its much simpler folk-origins. When Wolff and Hennings performed before the *karmapa*, or leader of a Tibetan Buddhist monastery in Sikkim, he declared the music to be 'the sound of the Void', and indeed it captures a uniquely mysterious quality not found elsewhere in the genre.

The first album of music, titled simply *Tibetan Bells*, was recorded in 1971 and was very much the prototype for *Tibetan Bells II*, released a decade later. On the more recent album, the beautiful resonances of the bells are used to conjure a musical atmosphere appropriate to the *Bardo* visions experienced at death and described in the *Tibetan Book of the Dead*. The album opens with music depicting the severance of the spirit from the body and progresses with compositions relating to the soul's journey on the inner planes. It culminates with a sequence in which, to quote Henry Wolff, 'in its transcendent aspect of pure, abstract vibration, Spirit sets out on its final journey through the Void, across the vast expanse of the universe.'

Needless to say, in a survey such as this there are inevitably musicians who have not been mentioned and works of flair and imagination that have been glossed over. However, for the musical enthusiast and meditator alike there is always the private joy of one's own discoveries — of finding musical compositions which then acquire special significance or which seem to have lain forever awaiting a receptive audience, and for this reason I make no apology for my omissions. Despite the fact that the musical selection presented here is very much one of individual choice, I hope, nevertheless, that the descriptions in the previous pages convey some feeling of the enormous variety of contemporary music available. From my own viewpoint the excitement rests in the fact that much of this wonderful music also has a practical application — as an accompaniment for inner journeys of the mind.

MUSIC AND THE ELEMENTS

There are many ways of classifying music and, in particular, its relationship to states of consciousness. The musician and author

Peter Michael Hamel, author of *Through Music to the Self*, presents a format of analysis, for example, which is strongly influenced by the Pythagorean concept of the 'Harmony of the Spheres', with its emphasis on acoustic proportions and ratios. For Hamel the mathematical symbolism of musical notation is part of esoteric tradition, manifesting in later periods in the thinking of Jesuit mystic Athanasius Kircher, the English Rosicrucian Robert Fludd and the German anthroposophist Rudolf Steiner. As Hamel indicates, the notes of the musical scale and the principles of harmonics can be analysed in terms of the Pythagorean monochord and for this writer 'basic laws reveal the connection between notes and numbers: the intervals can be physically experienced, and the ratios correspond to particular feelings'.[11]

Steven Halpern takes a comparable view in his book *Tuning the Human Instrument*, where he describes a correspondence between notes of the scale, colours of the spectrum and Kundalini chakras. Halpern's correspondences are as follows:

Note	Colour	Kundalini Chakra
C	Red	Muladhara
D	Orange	Svadisthana
E	Yellow	Manipura
F	Green	Anahata
G	Blue	Visuddha
A	Indigo	Ajna
B	Violet	Sahasrara

The main difficulty with Halpern's system is that, although it works neatly as a harmonic progression, it does not match the vibratory colours actually used by practitioners of Kundalini Yoga (see *Kundalini Yoga* in Chapter Four). It also has the drawback of imposing a framework which is not based on the actual belief system itself.

Fortunately there does seem to be a solution to the problem, and that is to employ the symbolic divisions of the elements: Earth, Water, Fire, Air and Spirit. This division has the advantage that it is used both in the Eastern and Western esoteric traditions — in Kundalini Yoga, in Western magic, in astrology and in the Tarot — and it enables us to discover corresponding music not on the basis of harmonics but through associated visual imagery. As a meditative tool it then becomes possible to produce a catalogue of music which has Earth-associations, Water-associations, Fire-associations and so on. These are not proposed as absolutes in the same way that fixed harmonic ratios are presented, but could be said to 'work' if, for the person in question, they are effective in evoking to consciousness the elemental imagery which is being used in the meditation. As we then go on our inner journeys of the mind and spirit, the music which is played as an accompaniment enhances the experiential reality we find ourselves in. *The music actually helps to create the mythic worlds we wish to enter.*

As an example of how this system can work I would like at this stage to propose a list of suggested correspondences between music and the five elements while recognising that this is very much a result of my own perceptual orientation. As I suggest in the workshop section of this chapter, readers should of course make their own list of music that is effective *for them* in bringing specific images before the mind's eye. Once again, I am confining my selection to music from the 'inner space' genre — however, in music there are no boundaries, and choices can be made from any type of music that seems personally appropriate for a given meditation or visualisation exercise. The choice is necessarily an individual one for each person undertaking the inner journey.

SOURCE-LIST: MUSIC FOR INNER SPACE

MUSIC FOR ENTERING AN ALTERED STATE (GENERAL):

Peter Baumann, 'Meadow of Infinity' (Part One), 'The Glass Bridge' and 'Meadow of Infinity' (Part Two), from *Romance 76* (Virgin)

Cluster & Eno, 'Ho Renomo' from *Cluster & Eno* (Sky)

Lol Creme and Kevin Godley, 'Fireworks', 'Burial Scene' (instrumental sequences only), 'Sleeping Earth' and 'The Flood' from *Consequences* (Mercury)

Eno, Moebius and Roedelius, 'Foreign Affairs' from *After the Heat* (Sky)

Philip Glass, *Koyaanisqatsi* (entire album)(Island)

Philip Glass, 'Part I' from *Music in 12 Parts* (Virgin)

Jon Hassell and Brian Eno, 'Charm' from *Possible Musics Vol. I* (EG/Polygram)

Gyorgy Ligeti, 'Requiem' and 'Lux Aeterna' from *2001* soundtrack (MGM)

Herbie Mann, 'Shomyo (Monks' Chant)', from *Gagaku & Beyond* (Finnadar)

Jay Moxham (Japetus), *The Great, Great Silence* (entire cassette)(Listen Music)

Klaus Schulze, 'Voices of Syn' from *Blackdance* (Virgin)

Klaus Schulze, 'Trancefer' (Side One) from *Trancefer* (Innovative Communication)

MUSIC FOR THE ELEMENT EARTH:

Chaitanya Hari Deuter, *Ecstasy* (entire album) (Kuckuck)

Brian Eno, *Ambient Four: On Land* (entire album) (EG/Polygram)

Philip Glass, 'Koyaanisqatsi' from *Koyaanisqatsi* (Island)

Michael Hoenig, 'Hanging Garden Transfer' from *Departure from the Northern Wasteland* (Warner Bros.)

Paul Horn, 'Psalm 4 — Enlightenment' from *Inside the Great Pyramid* (Mushroom)

Kitaro, 'Cosmic Energy' from *Oasis* (Kuckuck)

Jade Warrior, 'Waves Part II' (first third) from *Waves* (Island)

Herbie Mann, 'Shomyo' from *Gagaku & Beyond* (Finnadar)

Rajneesh Foundation musicians, 'Nadabrahma' (first two-thirds) from *Nataraj/Nadabrahma* (Rajneesh Foundation International)

Klaus Schulze, 'Conphara' and 'Chromengel' from *Cyborg* (Ohr), 'Ways of Changes' from *Blackdance* (Virgin), 'Spielglocken' from *Audentity* (Innovative Communication), 'A Few Minutes After Transfer' from *Trancefer* (Innovative Communication)

Tangerine Dream, 'The Big Sleep in Search of Hades' from *Stratosfear* (Virgin), 'Mysterious Semblance at the Strand of Nightmares' from *Phaedra* (Virgin), 'Ricochet, Part I' from *Ricochet* (Virgin), 'Rubycon, Part I' from *Rubycon* (Virgin), 'Alpha Centauri' from *Alpha Centauri* (Ohr), 'Nebulous Dawn' from *Zeit* (Ohr/Virgin), 'Through Metamorphic Rocks' from *Force Majeure* (Virgin), 'Tangram Set 2' from *Tangram* (Virgin)

Yatha Sidhra, 'Part I' from *Meditation Mass* (Brain/Metronome)

MUSIC FOR THE ELEMENT WATER:

Ash Ra Tempel, 'Jenseits' from *Join Inn* (Ohr)

Brian Eno, *Ambient One: Music for Airports* (first half, first side)(EG/Polygram), *Discreet Music* (first side)(Antilles), 'Inland Sea' and 'Sparrowfall I' from *Music for Films* (EG/Polygram)

Brian Eno and Harold Budd, 'Above Chiang Mai' and 'An Arc of Doves' from *Ambient Two: The Plateaux of Mirror* (EG/Polygram)

Fripp and Eno, 'Wind on Water' from *Evening Star* (Island)

Steve Hillage, 'Garden of Paradise' from *Rainbow Dome Musick* (Virgin)

Jade Warrior, 'Waterfall' and 'Memories of a Distant Sea' from *Floating World* (Island)

Kitaro, 'Oasis' from *Oasis* (Kuckuck)

Larkin, 'Emergence' from *O'cean* (Wind Sung Sounds)

Edgar Froese, 'Aqua' and 'Upland' from *Aqua* (Virgin), 'Epsilon in Malaysian Pale' from *Epsilon in Malaysian Pale* (Virgin)

Herbie Mann, 'Mauve over Blues' from *Gagaku & Beyond* (Finnadar)

Pink Floyd, 'Echoes' (first quarter) from *Meddle* (Harvest), 'Part Seven' from *Wish You Were Here* (Harvest)

Klaus Schulze, 'Bayreuth Return' from *Timewind* (Virgin), 'Crystal Lake' from *Mirage* (Island), 'Mindphaser' (first half) from *Moondawn* (Brain/Metronome), 'Nowhere — Now Here' from *Body Love* (Island)

MUSIC FOR THE ELEMENT FIRE:

Ash Ra, 'Sun Rain' from *New Age of Earth* (Virgin)

Manual Gottsching, 'Echo Waves' from *Invention for Electric Guitar* (Ohr)

Philip Glass, 'The Grid' from *Koyaanisqatsi* (Island)

Kitaro, 'Morning Prayer' from *Oasis* (Kuckuck)

Laraaji, 'Dance 1' and 'Dance 2' from *Ambient Three: Day of Radiance* (EG/Polygram)

Mike Oldfield, 'Part I' from *Ommadawn* (Virgin), 'Incantations Part 3' from *Incantations* (Virgin)

Klaus Schulze, 'Ways of Changes' from *Blackdance* (Virgin), 'Floating' from *Moondawn* (Brain/Metronome)

Tangerine Dream, 'Force Majeure' (last third) from *Force Majeure* (Virgin), 'Set 1' (first third) from *Tangram* (Virgin), 'Logos' (second half) and 'Logos 2' (middle section) from *Logos* (Virgin)

MUSIC FOR THE ELEMENT AIR:

Brian Eno, 'Under Stars' and 'Weightless' from *Apollo* (EG/Polygram)

Brian Eno and Harold Budd, 'The Chill Air' and 'Wind in Lonely Fences' from *Ambient Two: The Plateaux of Mirror* (EG/Polygram)

Fripp and Eno, 'Wind on Water' and 'Wind on Wind' from *Evening Star* (Island)

Michael Hoenig, 'Voices of Where' from *Departure from the Northern Wasteland* (Warner Bros.)

Paul Horn, 'Inside' and 'Mumtaz Mahal' from *Inside* (Epic), 'Psalm 2' and 'Psalm 3' (Initiation), 'Psalm 1' and 'Psalm 3' (Meditation), 'Psalm 2' (Enlightenment) and 'Psalm 4' (Fulfilment), from *Inside the Great Pyramid* (Mushroom)

Jade Warrior, 'Clouds' from *Floating World* (Island), 'The Wind Song' from *Kites* (Island)

Japetus, *The Great, Great Silence* (opening sequence)(Listen Music)

Herbert Joos, 'Why?' from *Daybreak* (Japo)

Larkin, 'Communitizing' from *O'cean* (Wind Sung Sounds)

Rajneesh Foundation musicians, 'Nadabrahma' (last third) from *Nataraj/Nadabrahma* (Rajneesh Foundation International)

Majo Rolyat, 'Sky Bells' from *Music Mantras* (Hermann Bauer Verlag)

Klaus Schulze, 'Wahnfried 1883' from *Timewind* (Virgin)

Jukka Tolonen, 'Mountains' from *Tolonen* (Sonet)

MUSIC FOR THE ELEMENT SPIRIT

Aeoliah and Larkin, *Inner Sanctum* (entire cassette)(Celestial Octaves)

Ash Ra, 'Ocean of Tenderness' from *New Age of Earth* (Virgin)

Jon Anderson, 'Song of Search' from *Olias of Sunhillow* (Atlantic)

Geoffrey Chandler, *Starscapes* (entire album)(Unity)

Cluster & Eno, 'Wehrmut' from *Cluster & Eno* (Sky)

Brian Eno, *Ambient One: Music for Airports* (last third of first side, second side), 'An Ending (Ascent)' and 'Stars' from *Apollo* (EG/Polygram)

Brian Eno and Harold Budd, 'Falling Light' from *Ambient Two: The Plateaux of Mirror* (EG/Polygram)

Fripp and Eno, 'An Index of Metals' (first quarter) from *Evening Star* (Island)

Edgar Froese, 'Epsilon in Malaysian Pale' (first half) from *Epsilon in Malaysian Pale* (Virgin)

Philip Glass, 'Prophecies' from *Koyaanisqatsi* (Island)

Manual Gottsching, 'Qasarsphere' from *Inventions for Electric Guitar* (Ohr)

Nancy Hennings and Henry Wolff, 'Astral Plane' from *Tibetan Bells II* (Celestial Harmonies)

Paul Horn, 'Akasha' from *Inside* (Epic)

Jade Warrior, 'Waves, Part II' (last third) from *Waves* (Island)

Larraaji, 'Meditation 1' from *Ambient Three: Day of Radiance* (EG/Polygram)

Gyorgy Ligeti, 'Requiem' and 'Lux Aeterna' from *2001* soundtrack (MGM)

Majo Roylat, 'Confidence' from *Music Mantras* (Hermann Bauer Verlag)

Klaus Schulze, 'Velvet Voyage' from *Mirage* (Island)

Tangerine Dream, 'Rubycon II' (first and last section) from *Rubycon* (Virgin), 'Sequent C' from *Phaedra* (Virgin), 'Sunrise in the 3rd System' from *Alpha Centauri* (Ohr), 'Atem' (second half) and 'Circulation of Events' from *Atem* (Ohr), 'Birth of Liquid Pleiades', 'Origin of Supernatural Probabilities' and 'Zeit' from *Zeit* (Ohr/Virgin)

MUSIC ENCOMPASSING ALL ELEMENTS:

Steve Hillage, 'For Ever Rainbow' from *Rainbow Dome Musick* (Virgin)

Klaus Schulze, 'Sebastian im Traum' from *Audentity* (Innovative Communication)

MUSIC FOR RELAXATION:

Robert Bearns and Ron Dexter, *Golden Voyage* (4 vols.)(Awakening Productions)

Jon Bernoff and Marcus Allen, *Breathe* (Whatever), *Petals* (Whatever)

Harold Budd, *The Pavilion of Dreams* (EG/Polygram)

Steven Halpern, *Dawn* (Halpern Sounds), *Eastern Peace* (Halpern Sounds), *Eventide* (Halpern Sounds), *Prelude* (Halpern Sounds), *Spectrum Suite* (Halpern Sounds), *Starborn Suite* (Halpern Sounds), *Zodiac Suite* (Halpern Sounds)

Bob Kindler, 'Music from the Matrix' (Jai Mai)

Kitaro, *Silk Road* (Kuckuck), *Ki* (Kuckuck), *Oasis* (Kuckuck), *Silver Cloud* (Polygram)

Majo Rolyat et al., *Music Mantras* (Hermann Bauer Verlag)

MISCELLANEOUS:

Colosseum, *Valentyne Suite* (Fontana)

Lol Creme and Kevin Godley, *Consequences* (Mercury)

Pink Floyd, *Meddle* (Harvest), *Ummagumma* (Harvest), *Wish You Were Here* (Harvest)

(For additional listings consult Anna Turner and Stephen Hill, *The Hearts of Space Guide*, P.O. Box 31321, San Francisco, California 94131)

WORKSHOP
MUSIC AND THE ELEMENTS

We have already explored the division of inner space music into the elements: Earth, Water, Fire, Air and Spirit (see album listing). The most important factor, of course, is to find music which evokes these associations *for you.*

— Explore your own record and cassette collection and draw up lists of music which appeal to you for meditation. Make a list for each element and then test the music in a meditation session.

— Having selected music that appeals to you, you may wish to make compilation tapes for each element by transferring the music onto a new cassette (C90 cassettes are ideal since they provide 45 minutes per side, which allows for an extended meditation session without interruption).

— You can also make compilation tapes of music associated with different emotions. Make one for *negative* feelings: anger, tension, fear, guilt, jealousy and so on, and another for *positive* feelings: inner peace, love, a balanced sense of purpose, clear resolve, compassion . . . Tapes can also be made which will assist in transforming a negative emotional state into a positive one. The pattern could look like this:

Process	*Appropriate Music*
Focusing personal awareness	'Ocean of Tenderness' from Ash Ra, *New Age of Earth*
Acknowledging a state of inner tension	'Vessels' from Philip Glass, *Koyaanisqatsi*
Draining the energy from the tension	'Cloudscape' from Philip Glass, *Koyaanisqatsi*
Affirming a sense of balance and purpose in life	Brian Eno, *Music for Airports* (Side One)
Relaxation and reflection	Steven Halpern, *Eventide*

Musical taste is very much a personal matter and everyone is uniquely different in what appeals. Make your own lists and compilation tapes to suit your own requirements, and if you are helping a friend, respect the fact that their musical taste may differ from your own.

When making your own compilation tapes try to avoid sudden stops and jarring noises. Phase gradually out of one musical sequence and lead gently into the next, so there are no bridging sounds to provide distractions when you are meditating.

Note This book does not advocate the practice of infringing musical copyright. Readers are urged to purchase the recommended music rather than re-record from other sources. International copyright law is vague in relation to private re-recording but in line with recent decisions protecting the act of private home video recording it seems a reasonable interpretation that you are not infringing copyright if the compilation tapes you make are for your personal use only, and not for resale.

PART TWO
MYTH & COSMOS

CHAPTER FOUR

SELF-INITIATION

In both West and East, profound esoteric systems have evolved to allow access to mystical states of consciousness. Although these systems are often regarded as 'secret traditions' and are generally veiled in complex symbolism the essential processes they describe are remarkably similar: each describes in a metaphorical way an entire cosmology and, by extension, a range of symbolic processes for the attainment of inner wholeness.

Each of these systems is archetypal and can be accessed by visualisation and meditation. In the following pages the background and cosmology of each tradition is discussed and the basic symbolism explored. Suggestions will also be offered for accompanying music and visualisation exercises to assist in tapping the profound 'inner spaces' available through these esoteric systems. All of these are authentic 'maps of consciousness' for, in presenting us with a range of archetypal symbols and processes, they allow us to explore our inner potential.

THE KABBALAH AND THE TREE OF LIFE

Taking its name from a Hebrew word meaning 'to receive from mouth to ear', the Kabbalah is the esoteric tradition of Judaism. The Kabbalah provides a mystical framework for understanding the Creation process described more literally in *Genesis* and clarifies the symbolic relationship between the domain of the Godhead (represented by the sacred name JHVH) and the archetypal man, Adam Kadmon.

The earliest Kabbalistic document is regarded as the book *Bahir*, first published in southern France *circa* 1176 AD, although the central work is the *Zohar* or *Book of Splendour*, ascribed to the Spanish mystic Moses de Leon and compiled *circa* 1286 AD. Because the Kabbalah was, and to a large extent still is, an oral tradition, it is difficult to say with certainty how ancient it is. However, the basic meditative approach is inherent in the central motif of the Tree of

AIN SOPH AUR
AUN SOPH
AIN

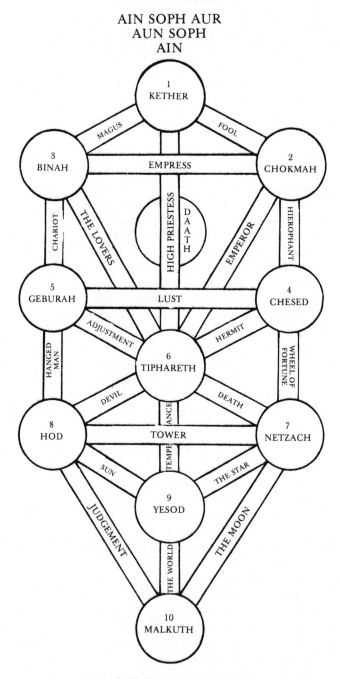

Tree of Life showing Tarot paths

Life which, like the *chakra* framework of Kundalini Yoga, provides us with a 'map' of inner man.

The Tree of Life consists of ten spheres through which the divine energy of the Godhead is manifest. These spheres, or *sephiroth*, align themselves in three columns headed by the Kabbalistic counterpart of the Trinity; *Kether, Chokmah* and *Binah*, often known as the Supernals. Since Judaism is monotheistic the *sephiroth* should be regarded as facets or manifestations of the One God, but as we will see later the Tree of Life provides us with a framework for correlating the deities of many different pantheons and this is one of its main functions in modern Western magic.

TRADITIONAL KABBALAH

From the Kabbalistic viewpoint the ongoing existence of man and Nature are a manifestation of a cosmic process which unfolds by stages and degrees, and which is symbolised on the Tree of Life by the following *sephiroth*:

KETHER   *The Crown* or peak of Creation
CHOKMAH   *Wisdom* (The Great Father)
BINAH   *Understanding* (The Great Mother)
CHESED   *Mercy*
GEBURAH   *Severity* or *Strength*
TIPHARETH   *Beauty* or *Harmony* (The Divine Son)
NETZACH   *Victory*
HOD   *Splendour*
YESOD   *The Foundation*
MALKUTH   *Kingdom* or *Earth* (The Divine Daughter)

The Crown resides at the top of the Tree, at a level which transcends duality. In this sense it parallels the Yogic state of *Nirvana* — encompassing direct experience of the Godhead. *Kether* is followed by *Chokmah*, the dynamic, creative force of the Trinity which is personified as the Great Father. *Binah*, the Great Mother, is the recipient of energy from *Chokmah* and is the womb from which all is born: symbolically she is the mother of us all.

Below the Trinity we find seven further *sephiroth* representing the Seven Days of Creation. According to Kabbalistic cosmology man was separated from the Godhead by the Fall, and the gulf between the first three *sephiroth* and the rest of the Tree is known as the Abyss. Accordingly the manifested universe takes a more accessible form in the *sephiroth* below this level.

Chesed and *Geburah* represent the Father of the world as we know it, in his two major aspects as a merciful ruler and as a destroyer respectively. Essentially *Chesed* maintains peace and order in the cosmos while *Geburah* breaks things down once their use is past.

Below them we come to *Tiphareth*, which resides in the centre of the Tree. As can be seen from its location, it lies midway between man and Godhead and thus represents the god-man: the spiritual being within each of us. The aim of all spiritual philosophies is to allow man to become the child of the gods, and so *Tiphareth* is the Son. *Tiphareth* also mediates between *Chesed* and *Geburah*, resolving their opposition in harmony.

Descending the Tree we now come to *Netzach*, which is a lower manifestation of *Chesed* and is generally correlated with the qualities of love and the emotions. *Hod*, directly opposite on the Tree, personifies the rational intellect and reason, and is a lower form of *Geburah*. *Yesod* resolves the second triad below the Abyss and on the body of Adam Kadmon corresponds to the genitals. Kabbalists regard *Yesod* as the seat of the animal soul, *Nephesch*, and consider it the source of fertility and sexuality. The final *sephirah*, *Malkuth*, is the feminine counterpart of *Tiphareth* — personified as the Daughter. Symbolic of the world as we know it, she is also the 'Spirit in Exile' and represents the feminine counterpart of God, the *Shekinah*.

Over and above this complex division of the ten *sephiroth*, the Kabbalists also divide the Tree of Life into four major planes of creative manifestation. The highest of these is the spiritual level called *Atziluth*, the world of archetypes, the very essence of all created forms. Beneath this plane, in *Briah*, these archetypes begin to crystallise into specific ideas, and in *Yetzirah* definite forms appear whose counterparts are the images of the unconscious mind. In the fourth world, *Assiah*, the manifesting forms of creation finally become 'real' on a physical level. However, it is very much a case of the reality of physical appearances.

Man as a created being necessarily has a spiritual counterpart on all of these levels but his limited awareness prevents him from experiencing the different planes of consciousness at will, and from integrating such knowledge into his concept of himself. The act of spiritual awakening involves knowledge of man's inner self — in fact knowledge of his 'soul'. In the Kabbalah the soul is divided into three aspects: *Neschamah, Ruach* and *Nephesch*. These equate with different *sephiroth* so that *Neschamah*, for example, corresponds to *Kether, Chokmah* and *Binah*, while the *Ruach* encompasses the *sephiroth* from *Chesed* to *Hod*. The *Nephesch* aspect of the soul, as we have already seen, is identified with *Yesod*.

OCCULT KABBALAH
The magicians of the Hermetic Order of the Golden Dawn expanded the traditional concept of the Tree of Life so that it encompassed other pantheons as well — thereby taking in all of the

major gods and goddesses of the Western mystery tradition. They also structured their rituals to commence with the lowest *sephirah*, Malkuth, and progressively ascend the Tree towards the Godhead. If we thus regard the Tree of Life as a framework for exploring the mythic sources of the Western psyche the structure which emerges is something like this:

First Level
Malkuth
Associated with the Earth, crops, the immediate environment, living things. Ideas have their materialisation here and all journeys of an 'inner' nature begin here. In Roman mythology the entrance to the Underworld was through a cave near Naples, and symbolically Malkuth is the entrance through Earth to the unconscious mind.

Mythological Images: Persephone (Greek), Proserpine (Roman), Geb (Egyptian)

Second Level
Yesod
Associated with the Moon, Yesod, like Malkuth, is a predominantly feminine sphere. It is both the recipient of impulses from the higher astral plane and the transmitter of sexual energies into a more tangible physical form in Malkuth. Consequently it is a domain which abounds with astral imagery and is appropriately associated with the element Water.

Yesod is the seat of the sexual instinct, corresponding with the genital *chakra* of the microcosmic man. It is also the sphere of subconscious activity stimulated through sexual magic and is the symbolic domain most clearly identified with witchcraft. Wiccan rites are essentially a form of lunar worship.

Mythological Images: Hecate, Artemis, Luna, Diana, Selene, Bast

Third Level
Hod
Associated with the planet Mercury, representing intellect and rational thinking, Hod is a lower aspect of the Great Father, for Mercury is the messenger of the gods. As the next stage beyond Yesod it represents in some measure the conquest of the animal instincts, albeit at an intellectual rather than on an emotional and intuitive level. Hod is the structuring principle in our immediate universe: a *sephirah* which embodies order and logical categories. It is in this capacity that we perceive God the Architect manifesting in a world of myriad forms and structures.

Mythological Images: Hermes, Mercury, Anubis

91

Fourth Level
Netzach
Associated with the planet Venus, Netzach complements Hod and represents the arts, creativity, subjectivity, intuition and the emotions. It is essentially outgoing rather than introspective, however, and its instinctual drive can be contrasted with the sombre, constrained qualities of Hod. Netzach is the sphere of love and spiritual passion and from a mythic viewpoint is the source of the beauty of natural living forms.
Mythological Images: Aphrodite, Venus, Hathor

Fifth Level
Tiphareth
Just as Hod and Netzach are opposites, so too are Yesod and Tiphareth — the embodiments of Moon and Sun, and feminine and masculine polarities respectively. If Yesod represents the animal instincts, Tiphareth is the mediating stage between man and Godhead on the mystical ascent. It is here that man experiences spiritual rebirth. His psyche now blends both its emotional and rational aspects and his aspirations are towards higher being. Tiphareth is associated with deities of rebirth and resurrection and, in a cosmological sense, with the Sun as giver of life and light. Man catches for the first time a glimpse of his Father beyond the Abyss — above form and imagery — and the first rays of god-awareness are aroused in him. Tiphareth is also the sphere of sacrifice, for the old restricted and unenlightened personality is offered in place of new understanding and insight. Man for the first time begins to operate through a spiritual vehicle.
Mythological Images: Apollo, Osiris, Mithra, Christ

Sixth Level
Geburah
Associated with Mars, traditionally a god of war, Geburah represents severity and justice. The energies of Geburah are absolutely impartial, since there can be no flaw of sentiment in the eye of a wise ruler. The destructive forces of this sphere are intended as a purging, cleansing force and are positive in their application. It thus embodies a spiritual vision of power operating in the universe to destroy unwanted and unnecessary elements after their usefulness has passed. As an aspect of the Father, Geburah shows discipline and precision in his destructiveness. His mission on the battlefield of the cosmos is to inculcate a rational economy of form which in its lower aspect is reflected in Hod.
Mythological Images: Ares, Mars, Horus

Seventh Level
Chesed
Associated with Jupiter, Chesed is the other face of the destructive ruler, representing divine mercy and majesty. In the same way that Geburah breaks down forms, Chesed is protective and tends to reinforce and consolidate. It maintains the potency of the Great Father beyond the Abyss, which it reflects on a lower, while still exalted, scale. Whereas Mars rides in his chariot, Chesed/Jupiter is seated on a throne, overviewing his kingdom. He produces a stabilising influence and mythologically helps to channel abstract potentialities into more specific forms.

From a psychological viewpoint Chesed represents the highest point in the Collective Unconscious for beyond him no images are really appropriate. However, all esoteric systems tend to preserve a sense of the visual metaphor.
Mythological Images: Zeus, Jupiter, Ra

Eighth Level
Binah
The first of the Supernals beyond the Abyss, Binah represents the Great Mother in all her forms. She is the 'womb of forthcoming', the source of all great and sacred images and forms which enter the manifested universe as archetypes. She is also the supreme female principle in the creation process and as such is invariably the mother of the god-man or messiah who intervenes between man and God. Binah is thus associated with the Virgin Mary, mother of Christ in Tiphareth, but also with Rhea and Isis. In a more tangible way she is sometimes the spouse of the ruler of the archetypal world. A classic example is Demeter — the wife of Zeus and the mother of Persephone.
Mythological Images: Rhea, Demeter, Isis, The Virgin Mary

Ninth Level
Chokmah
The next of the Trinitarian god-images is that of the Great Father. Chokmah provides the seminal spark of life which is potency only until it enters the womb of Binah. From the union of Father and Mother come forth all the images of creation. Associated with the ancient gods beyond the known universe, Chokmah is represented by deities like Kronos and Thoth, who sustain the very basis of existence.
Mythological Images: Kronos, Saturn, Thoth, Ptah

Tenth Level
Kether
This stage of consciousness represents the first dawning of creation from beyond the veils of non-existence (called in the Kabbalah *Ain Soph Aur* — 'the Limitless Light'). Upon the Tree of Life Kether lies on the Middle Pillar and it therefore transcends all notions of duality. Sometimes associated with the Heavenly Androgyne — a symbol of the union of opposites — it represents a level of sublime neutrality. Kether has few appropriate representations in the classical pantheons and is far removed from the world of mankind in Malkuth.

Mythological Images: Aion, Abraxas, The Heavenly Androgyne

These are the major levels of consciousness delineated in the Kabbalah and they represent a progression from animal-man, to god-man, to Godhead. However, as John Lilly has pointed out, it is wise to regard these and subsequent esoteric systems as profound symbolic metaphors. The Kabbalah allows a systematic and orderly mystical ascent, and as in Kundalini Yoga, approaches the furthest reaches of human consciousness with respect and awe.

VIBRATING THE SACRED NAMES
As we saw in an earlier chapter of this book, the vibration of sound is considered universally to represent the 'coming into being' of manifested forms. Sound literally creates the universe.

In the Kabbalah each of the *sephiroth* of the Tree of Life were additionally given god-names — Hebrew words relating to different aspects of divinity. From a meditative viewpoint these represent the mantras appropriate to each level of consciousness. The ten god-names are as follows:

Kether: *Ehieh* — pronounced *Eee-Heee-Yeh*
Chokmah: *JHVH* (Jehovah, Yahweh) — pronounced *Ye-Ho-Waaa*
Binah: *JHVH Elohim* — pronounced *Ye-Ho-Waaa Eloheeem*
Chesed: *El* — pronounced *Elll . . .*
Geburah: *Elohim Gibor* — pronounced *Eloheeem Giiborrr*
Tiphareth: *JHVH Aloah Va Daath* — pronounced *Ye-Ho-Waaa Aloaaa Vaaa Daaath*
Netzach: *JHVH Tzabaoth* — pronounced *Ye-Ho-Waaa Tzaabayoth*
Hod: *Elohim Tzabaoth* — pronounced *Eloheeem Tzaabayoth*
Yesod: *Shaddai El Chai* — pronounced *Sha-Dai El Haiii*
Malkuth: *Adonai Ha Aretz* — pronounced *Aaa-Doh-Naii Haaa Aaaretz*

COLOURS OF THE SEPHIROTH
In modern magical applications of the Kabbalah the ten sephiroth

have also been correlated with colours and it is important to know these, since they are obviously a vital part of the visualistic process. The following were known in the Hermetic Order of the Golden Dawn as the Queen Scale of Colours:

Kether: Brilliant White
Chokmah: Grey
Binah: Black
Chesed: Blue
Geburah: Red
Tiphareth: Golden Yellow
Netzach: Emerald Green
Hod: Orange
Yesod: Purple/Indigo
Malkuth: A combination of Citrine, Olive, Russet and Black

These colours, of course, correlate to some extent with the mythic figures who are ascribed to these spheres. Chesed, the *sephirah* of the ruler-deities of the sky, is appropriately blue, while Geburah, the domain of the warlike gods, is red. Solar deities are invariably equated with Tiphareth, which is golden yellow. However, when one adds to the Tree the so-called eleventh *sephirah, Daath,* which is positioned on the Abyss, the colours form a rainbow mandala.

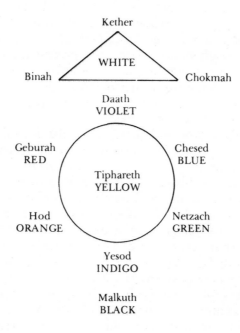

Netzach then becomes green — the complementary colour of the *sephirah*, Geburah, which lies diagonally opposite — and Hod becomes orange because of its diagonal relationship to Chesed. Yesod (indigo) and Daath (violet) complete the spectrum. The Supernals, as the supreme state of spiritual consciousness, can then be collectively represented as brilliant white, while Malkuth becomes collectively black. This colour system is, in fact, the one used in the Golden Dawn visualisation procedure known as the Middle Pillar exercise, which is described in the workshop section.

VISIONARY ASPECTS OF THE KABBALAH

From a shamanic point of view the purest expression of visionary Kabbalah is found in the early, first century school of Hekhaloth and Merkabah mysticism. The *hekhaloth* were the 'halls of God's palace' through which the mystic had to pass in order to reach God's throne, or chariot (*merkabah*).

It seems that there were many ways of ascending through the *hekhaloth*. These included fasting, prayers, visualisation and the singing of hymns. The mystic also made use of talismans and magical seals, and knew the passwords for each of the palace gates he wished to enter.

In the early Kabbalistic cosmology there was a clear distinction between the domains where one obtained spiritual grace and mystical knowledge and the terrifying and hostile powers which guarded these sacred precincts. According to the text of the *Greater Hekhaloth*, for example, the Lord God of the seventh heaven is protected by 'mighty ones, terrifying, powerful, fearsome . . . sharp swords are in their hands, flashing lightning shoots from their eyes, streams of fire come from their nostrils, and burning coals from their mouths. They are garbed with helmet and armour, with spears and lances hanging at their sides'.[1]

Although the major works of the Kabbalah are theoretical rather than practical it is possible to piece together the general approach to meditation, in terms of techniques. We know from the writings of the 13th century Kabbalist Abraham ben Samuel Abulafia that he advocated intoning the god-name so that its energy coursed through the 'chariot' of the body, producing a state of mystical enlightenment. Abulafia would actually visualise the god-name in the form of a chariot and regarded its constituent letters as the key to spiritual knowledge: 'See them also as the strings of a violin which vibrate as the bow passes over them,' he advised, 'and let them quicken your soul's innately divine music in the same way.'[2]

The 16th century practitioner Rabbi Joseph Tzayach similarly practised a form of meditation combining colour visualisation and the intonation of sacred letter-combinations. The god-names of the *sephiroth* were also incorporated into a prayer.

For the Merkabah mystic, however, fewer details of specific techniques are available. It seems that the initial task was to pass through the first six heavenly halls using a combination of sacred names, magical talismans and visualisations to gain admittance. If the devotee was sufficiently knowledgeable and pure in intent he would then be granted entry to the seventh hall. Here the throne would appear in the form of a chariot and lift him in ecstasy to the transcendent realms of the highest heavens. In the Merkabah tradition the flight of Ezekiel and the vision of Elijah epitomised this process. In *Ezekiel* 1:4 we read, 'I saw, and behold a stormy wind coming from the north, a great cloud and flashing fire, a glow round about, and from its midst, a vision of the Speaking Silence, in the midst of the fire'. Ezekiel then describes the four angelic beings who emerged from the fire and relates how he fell on his face before the throne of the Lord. In Elijah's vision (2 *Kings* 2:11) a similar phenomenon occurs: 'There appeared a chariot of fire, and horses of fire . . . and Elijah went to heaven in a stormy wind . . .'

According to the distinguished Kabbalist Aryeh Kaplan the 'Speaking Silence' referred to above is the seventh heavenly hall, which marks the spiritual barrier between Good and Evil. Similarly Leo Schaya, in his *Universal Meaning of the Kabbalah*, identifies the seventh heaven as Chesed, the highest of the *sephiroth* beneath the Supernals and the Abyss. It would seem therefore that, in essence, the Merkabah mystics were ascending through the lower seven spheres of what was later formalised as the Tree of Life, and then transporting themselves in the heavenly chariot to the mystical transcendence of Binah, Chokmah and beyond.

In the Golden Dawn, similar techniques of Kabbalistic visualisation were used to rise on the 'inner planes'. In Flying Roll XI, MacGregor Mathers describes a technique for combining visualisation and magical will to move in the trance state from one sphere of the Tree to the next:

'Rising on the planes is a spiritual process after spiritual conceptions and higher aims; by concentration and contemplation of the Divine, you formulate a Tree of Life passing from you to the spiritual realms above and beyond you. Picture to yourself that you stand in Malkuth — then by use of the Divine Names and aspirations you strive upward by the Path of Tau towards Yesod, neglecting the crossing rays which attract you as you pass up. Look upwards to the Divine Light shining down from Kether upon you. From Yesod leads up the Path of Temperance, Samekh, the arrow cleaving upward leads the way to Tiphareth, the Great Central Sun of Sacred Power.'[3]

In this practical statement Mathers demonstrates a specific visualisation technique for passing imaginally from Malkuth through Yesod to Tiphareth, identifying what is regarded as the 'Middle Pillar' ascension upon the central axis of the Tree of Life. There are, of course, ten spheres of the Tree to explore, not just those of the Middle Pillar. Seven of these *sephiroth* — the 'lower heavens' — are accessible through visualisation and magical will, while the final three transcendent states of consciousness are beyond the range of normal inner plane workings. Nevertheless, there is no doubt that the Kabbalistic Tree of Life provides one of the finest frameworks available for exploring the Western psyche.

WORKSHOP

THE KABBALAH AND THE TREE OF LIFE

STAGE ONE

Stand in the centre of a darkened room facing towards the East and relax the body progressively from the feet through to the head (see Workshop, Chapter One). Now, having focused awareness in the head, imagine large vibrant balls of white light in the four quarters and in their centres visualise a personal symbol for each of the four elements in turn:

In the East: Air (clouds in the sky)
In the South: Fire (a darting flame)
In the West: Water (a flowing stream)
In the North: Earth (rocks, plants)

Now also visualise a large vibrant ball of white light above you, representing Spirit, and feel its energies pouring down onto the crown of your head. Imagine this vibrant light entering your head, as if you were a hollow vessel, and visualise it passing down through the central axis of your body to your feet. As the energy descends it activates the following centres in turn:

Head: Visualise radiant white light
Throat: Visualise mauve light
Heart: Visualise golden yellow light
Genitals: Visualise purple light
Feet: Visualise black intensity

STAGE TWO

After you have become proficient in this visualisation you may like to plan the following as a sequel. It will require your own selection of music, so make a compilation tape allowing 3-5 minutes for each element and ensure that they follow in the correct order. If you wish you can also vibrate the traditional Kabbalistic mantras for each of the chakras in turn (for pronunciations see page 94).

We are now endeavouring to raise our energy from Earth-consciousness to Spirit-consciousness (Kether) so the direction is upwards through the body and out through the crown of the head, embracing the Universe.

First feel the ground beneath your feet, concentrate the energy in the black intensity of Malkuth and lift it progressively through your body, purifying and transforming it at each stage:

Feet Visualise black (Earth): *Adonai Ha Aretz*
Appropriate music: 'Hanging Garden Transfer' from Michael Hoenig, *Departure from the Northern Wasteland*

Genitals Visualise purple (Water): *Shaddai El Chai*
Appropriate music: 'Crystal Lake' from Klaus Schulze, *Mirage*
Heart Visualise golden yellow (Fire): *JHVH Aloah Va Daath*
Appropriate music: 'Dance Two' from Laraaji, *Days of Radiance (Ambient Three)*
Throat Visualise mauve (Air): *JHVH Elohim*
Appropriate music: 'The Great, Great Silence' (opening sequence) from Japetus, *The Great, Great Silence*, or 'Wahnfried 1883' (last quarter) from Klaus Schulze, *Timewind*
Head Visualise radiant white (Spirit): *Ehieh*
Appropriate music: 'Requiem' and 'Lux Aeterna' from Gyorgy Ligeti, *2001* film soundtrack

ADVANCED MEDITATION

First prepare a compilation tape which includes music for Earth (5 minutes), Air (5 minutes) and Spirit (5 minutes). Sit relaxed in a comfortable chair with your hands resting on your knees and close your eyes. Feel the solidity of your chair and imagine that, like a king or queen seated on a throne, you are surveying your domain — the world around you.

Now imagine that your throne is gradually transforming into a chariot. Wheels manifest on each side and two majestic winged horses appear before you — one white, the other black . . . They now prepare to draw your chariot up into the sky, taking you to the sacred world. Gradually you gather pace and momentum and it is like leaving your terrestrial, earth-bound personality behind as you soar away on an adventure of the spirit.

You can place your total trust in the horses drawing your chariot, for they are lifting you to higher, transcendental realms.

In choosing accompanying music, select compositions which incorporate the following characteristics:

Earth: solidity and balance (first phase), increasing momentum (second phase)
Appropriate music: 'Bayreuth Return' from Klaus Schulze, *Timewind*, or 'Trancefer' (Side One) from Klaus Schulze, *Trancefer*
Air: soaring qualities
Appropriate music: 'Wahnfried 1883' from Klaus Schulze, *Timewind*
Spirit: transcendence
Appropriate music: 'Song of Search' from Jon Anderson, *Olias of Sunhillow*, or 'An Ending (Ascent)' from Brian Eno, *Apollo*, or 'Rubycon Part Two' (opening and final sequence) from Tangerine Dream, *Rubycon*

Note It is possible to adapt this visualisation to incorporate the two Tarot cards *The Emperor* and *The Charioteer* (see section on The Tarot). The dominant elements of *The Emperor* are Earth and Fire. The Emperor is 'solid and dependable' and sits on a throne of red rock, surveying an essentially barren and unfriendly kingdom: volcanoes erupt with molten lava in the distance. He wears a cloak and armour of a reddish hue and looks vigilantly towards the horizon. His quality is *static*.

The Charioteer, on the other hand, is ruled by Binah (the Great Mother = Water) and some Tarot packs depict him in armour with a crab on his helmet. He surveys the world of forms from an airborne chariot so he incorporates the complementary elements Water and Air, and his quality is *dynamic*.

The above sequence for your musical accompaniment then becomes:

Earth (solidity and balance); Fire (momentum); Air (soaring qualities); Water (reflecting the world below) and Spirit (transcendence).

THE TAROT

For many people the 78 cards of the Tarot are associated with fortune-telling and gypsy folklore, and as symbols of popular culture they have appeared in feature films, novels and plays, and on graphic posters. Several contemporary rock-music albums have been based on motifs from the Tarot, and these symbols were also a source of visionary inspiration for the Nobel Prize winning poet and occultist William Butler Yeats. There have also been many theories concerning the Tarot — most of them fanciful. These include Antoine Court de Gebelin's notion that the Tarot originated in ancient Egypt as the 'secret book of Thoth', Etteilla's theory that the Magi created them 171 years after the Great Flood, and Paul Foster Case's claim that they were created by a band of adepts in Fez, Morocco, *circa* 1200 AD as a synthesis of the 'universal mystery teaching'.

De Gebelin first proposed the Egyptian origin of the Tarot in his extraordinary nine-volume work *Le Monde Primitif*, first published in Paris between 1775 and 1784. De Gebelin believed that the 22 cards of the Major Arcana — the pictorial trumps of the Tarot pack, as distinct from the 56 cards of the four suites — were in fact an ancient Egyptian text which had been rescued from the smouldering ruins of desecrated Egyptian temples. De Gebelin associated several of the cards with Egyptian deities, linking *The Star*, for example, to Isis, *The Devil* to Typhon and *The Charioteer* to Osiris. He also believed that the word 'Taro' was Egyptian for 'royal road of life' — a somewhat surprising assertion since at the time he was writing the Egyptian hieroglyphs had not yet been deciphered.

Etteilla, whose real name was Alliette, was a 19th century Parisian wig-maker and devotee of Pythagorean number-symbolism. Influenced strongly by De Gebelin he believed that the Tarot was written on gold leaf by 17 Magi, including a priest called Athotis, whom he took to be the great-grandson of Noah and a descendant of Mercury. He also maintained that the Tarot had originally been conceived by Hermes Trismegistos ('Thrice Greatest Hermes') and that this figurehead of the Western mystery tradition had inspired the Magi to compile the book in a temple near Memphis.

Paul Foster Case was certainly closer to the mark than his occult predecessors in dating the Tarot cards to the medieval period. However, like De Gebelin, he too was prone to pseudo-linguistics, asserting in his well known book *The Tarot* that the name 'Taro' could be arranged in different ways. The mock-Latin phrase 'Rota Taro Orat Tora Ator', for example, was said to translate as 'The Wheel of Tarot speaks the Law of Hathor' — another dubious and quite unfounded reference to the Egyptian origin of the Tarot. It should be reasonably obvious to anyone who studies the earliest Tarot decks that the cards are strongly medieval in inspiration. *The Fool* is clearly recognisable as a court-jester, *The Emperor* of the Venetian Tarot is very much a medieval monarch, and the early Mantegna Tarocchi card game, which certainly influenced later Tarot decks, included a medieval 'Artisan' and 'Merchant' alongside the Beggar (another version of *The Fool*), the Pope (*The Hierophant*) and the Imperator (*The Emperor*).

However, while links between the Tarot and earlier esoteric traditions cannot be established historically, it is clear that the cards of the Major Arcana do present an initiatory sequence. There is no doubt that, from a symbolic viewpoint, an important breakthrough came in the history of occult thought when 19th century French hermeticist Eliphas Levi correlated the Major Arcana of the Tarot and the sephiroth on the Tree of Life. Papus developed this even further, correlating specific cards of both the Major and Minor Arcana with each of the four letters of the sacred Tetragrammaton JHVH as well as with signs of the Zodiac. But if the Major Arcana and the Kabbalistic Tree of Life blend especially well together, it is not for historical reasons but rather because, like all authentic esoteric frameworks, the symbols have archtetypal significance and one would expect correspondences between any mystical systems purporting to describe the sacred and transpersonal images of the psyche.

In this way the 22 Major Arcana are examples of Jung's archetypes of the Collective Unconscious — they constitute a mythology of the mind. The symbolic figures presented on the different cards personify different facets of the psyche, some of them intuitive, loving and benevolent. Some mirror aspects of the archetypal Great Father and Great Mother and the Divine Son and Daughter, while *The Wheel of Fortune* is nothing other than a medieval mandala — symbol of the inner centre. As we will see, there are cards of spiritual growth — *Judgement, Justice* and *The Sun*, cards in which the 'dark' or 'animal' side of the psyche is encountered — *Death, The Devil, Strength*, and trumps of strong mystical purpose — *Temperance* and *The Hermit*. Finally there are cards of transcendence — *The Lovers* (in which sexual opposites blend together) and *The Fool* (who embraces Space).

In essence, then, the Major Arcana constitute an inner journey of the mind, delineating paths which can be followed meditatively if one is to communicate with the Higher Self. The following descriptions summarise the basic processes of the Major Arcana and also their 'position' on the Tree of Life — a correlation which is important in modern Western magic. Some readers may wish, however, to use the cards simply as they are — as a workable sequence of archetypal images which lead progressively through the psyche towards individuation and transcendence. The following sequence takes us through the Tarot images of the Major Arcana, from the entry point into the subconscious at the base of the Tree of Life, through to the highest point in *Kether*:[4]

THE WORLD (MALKUTH-YESOD)

This card represents the descent into the underworld — a theme characterised in Greek mythology by Persephone in Hades. However, death is the other side of life and Persephone symbolises the wheat grain which grows to maturity, is reaped and allows new seed to be sewn, in a perpetual cycle of harvest. Persephone dies to live again: her existence is manifest both in the realm of the living and the dead. In *The World* she is androgynous, representing both male and female polarities, despite her apparent femininity. She dances within a wreath of wheat grains, and around her are the symbols of the 'Fixed' signs of the Zodiac: Man (Aquarius); the Eagle (Scorpio); the Lion (Leo) and the Bull (Taurus). The path of *The World* is the first on the journey towards cosmic consciousness.

JUDGEMENT (MALKUTH-HOD)

A new personality has to be formed from the diverse and unharmonised aspects of unenlightened man: his entry into the 'inner world' heralds new possibility as he arises from the coffin of death and ignorance. The path of *Judgement* leads to Hod, representing rational intelligence, and the spiritual direction is towards mastering the irrational animal instincts. In some Tarot decks the figures are shown gesturing with their arms to form the pattern L V X: 'Light'. Gabriel, Angel of Divine Breath, revivifies them and they rise in triumph. On his trumpet he heralds *new being*.

THE MOON (MALKUTH-NETZACH)

This, too, points towards a new evolutionary phase. The lobster, representing an early form of life, is seen to emerge from the waters; the aggressiveness of the wolf has been tamed in the dog, and both look upwards towards Hecate, the Moon, to whom the dog was sacred. Water is the predominant element. Aphrodite, a goddess of the Netzach sphere, was said to have been born in the foam, and represents the White Goddess, the resplendent beauty of love and Nature. *The Moon* also represents the ebb and flow of tides: the cycles affecting man in his environment.

THE SUN (YESOD-HOD)

Beneath the Sun, in a magical ring, dance the young twins; a boy and girl embracing each other. They represent a type of innocence, and the synthesis of opposite polarities — a common theme in the Tarot. They are clearly ruled by the Sun, representing unity and vitality and the path of 'enlightenment', but a barrier (the wall) stands before their self-fulfilment.

This path is ruled by the archangel Michael, personification of Fire, who harshly disperses darkness and leaves no scope for self-delusion. However, the most rigorous trials of personal karma will occur further up the Tree in regions associated with the Dark Night of the Soul.

THE STAR (YESOD-NETZACH)

This card is associated with intuition, reflection, and the hidden qualities of Nature, represented by Netzach. The beautiful naked Goddess kneels by a pool pouring water from flasks held in both hands. She is an aspect of Mother Nature, a less transcendent and more accessible aspect of the Great Mother in Binah, and she looks thoughtfully upon the waters of universal consciousness which fertilise the earth world and inspire its human inhabitants. In his quest for the Grail of Enlightenment, man has to modify his own vessel of perception and allow himself to be filled by the waters of higher consciousness.

THE TOWER (HOD-NETZACH)

The Tower of Babel was an arrogant attempt by man to scale the heights of heaven. It is clear from this card that potentially *The Tower* reaches up to Kether, the crown of all being, if man can overcome his pride. This path reinforces and consolidates the polar opposites Hod and Netzach. *The Tower*, however, also represents the body, and the influx of divine energy — as in Kundalini Yoga — can produce a devastating and harmful effect if the personality is not sufficiently balanced and refined to receive it. *The Tower* is ruled by Mars, who ruthlessly destroys ignorance and limited, vain conceptions.

THE DEVIL (HOD-TIPHARETH)

We see demonic forms of man and woman bound by chains to a pedestal. Above them is a gloating devil. At this stage, the wanderer in inner space must take stock of his weaknesses, particularly those relating to worldly possessions and notions of security, because he is on the verge of his first spiritual transformation. Capricorn, the goat, represents darkness and bestiality. In some Tarot decks he has eagle-legs, parodying the union of opposites — Air and Earth — and typically, an inverted pentagram rests upon his brow, indicating the reverence of illusion rather than essence. However, *The Devil* really indicates the plight of man within his limited frameworks, and thus offers a definite lesson towards the gaining of inner unity.

DEATH (NETZACH-TIPHARETH)

Like *The Devil, Death* indicates man's shortcomings, and the limited, temporal nature of his personality. However, death is also the herald of new life, and behind the scythe-wielding skeleton-figure new light will dawn on the horizon. The scythe is associated with Kronos, the Greek founder deity, transcendent beyond time, and the path is called *Nun* in the Kabbalah — meaning 'a fish'. Christ was often symbolised by a fish ('I am a fisher of men . . .') and *Nun* leads into Tiphareth, a sphere of spiritual awakening and rebirth appropriate to the Christos consciousness. The path through death thus leads to regeneration.

TEMPERANCE (YESOD-TIPHARETH)

This card represents the line of direct mystical ascent from the level of the enclosed and limited personality to the more illuminated spiritual man. Raphael stands in the desert, representing the arid toil of the Dark Night of the Soul prior to spiritual fulfilment, and pours the waters of life from a Sun vessel into a Moon vessel. This constitutes a tempering, of union, of opposites: of male (solar) and female (lunar) energies. All aspects of the lower subconscious find their unity on this path, and each of the elements, Fire, Earth, Air and Water, is blended into one. Raphael bestows grace, and above him shines a rainbow — symbolising God's covenant with man. The new light of day dawns over a distant mountain.

One of the visions of *Temperance* is that of Sagittarius, the centaur, who combines man and animal. He fires his arrow into the air — thereby personifying aspiration and transition. We can follow the path of the golden arrow; Tiphareth, the sphere of god-man, is within reach.

THE HERMIT (TIPHARETH-CHESED)

Like the Ancient of Days, the Hermit is a bearded, patriarchal figure, although his splendour is shielded by the anonymity of his hooded cloak. Having reached Tiphareth the magician now proceeds to the loftier reaches of the Tree of Life. The path of *The Hermit* is ruled by Mercury, who is an aspect of Chokmah, and Thoth — the 'Great Father' archetypes of the Western mystery tradition. However, the path is also called *Yod*, ascribed to Virgo, showing that in some measure a unison of sexual polarities has been achieved. The Hermit slowly wends his way upwards towards the hazards and loneliness of the Abyss. However, he has achieved a profound state of self-realisation in the harmony of Tiphareth and his goal is firmly in his mind. A lamp representing his own inner light illumines his pathway.

JUSTICE (TIPHARETH-GEBURAH)

This is a karmic path demanding balance, adjustment and total self-evaluation. Ruled by Venus, it leads to the sphere of her lover Mars and is appropriately designated by the figure of the Goddess holding the scales and the sword of justice. She resembles Maat, the Egyptian personification of Truth who resided in the Osirian Hall of Judgement and weighed the heart of the deceased against a feather. Thoth, the great scribe, would record the verdict.

The shaman on this path encounters the visions of his own karma which thrive in the subconscious as images based upon negative power. Since in the Hall of Judgement only truth can be admitted, the magician cannot proceed to a higher sphere on the Tree of Life until retribution is made. As occult writer Gareth Knight notes, '. . . the ability to face up to the true situation within oneself, coupled with the willingness to change it . . . is a lot easier to say than it is to do, for it requires ruthless honesty, considerable powers of discernment, and much courage, but prolonged intention and aspiration'.[5] The task now is to obliterate pretence and the falsity associated with outward semblances, and rediscover the true, inner self.

THE HANGED MAN

THE HANGED MAN (HOD-GEBURAH)
This path, like that of *Justice*, leads to Geburah, the sphere of action. The Hanged Man swings by his foot, symbolising sacrifice, but because of his inverted position he is also like a reflection in water — the element ascribed to this path. His head is aglow and he seems to be transmitting light to lower levels of manifestation. The waters flow from Binah, the Great Mother who is the Ocean of All Being. The magical task is to become a vessel for the higher spiritual energies, and allow them to fill one's inner being.

STRENGTH (GEBURAH-CHESED)

This card, resting horizontally across the Tree, occupies an equivalent position to *The Tower*, but at a higher level. Whereas *The Tower* lies just below the so-called Veil of Paroketh, which separates the terrestrial personality from the higher self, *Strength* lies just below the Abyss, the gulf between individuality and universality. We are shown a woman — personifying intuition — prising open the jaws of a lion. This symbolises complete mastery over any remaining vestiges of the animal soul (Nephesch) and the ability to endure the karma of earlier stages of spiritual growth.

THE WHEEL OF FORTUNE

THE WHEEL OF FORTUNE (NETZACH-CHESED)

This card shows the mandala motif of the Western magical tradition. The Wheel of Fortune is a symbol of the inner center, and the 'tides of destiny' flow in either a positive or negative way according to our degree of personal attunement to the natural cycles of life.

The Wheel of Fortune leads to Chesed and understandably comes under the jurisdiction of Jupiter. Chesed is the region of pure archetypes, the realm of manifested existence closest to the world of Spirit beyond the Abyss. Since Kether is androgynous, we would expect, and do in fact find, both polarities featuring on this path, for the ultimate destiny of man is to transcend duality in all its forms.

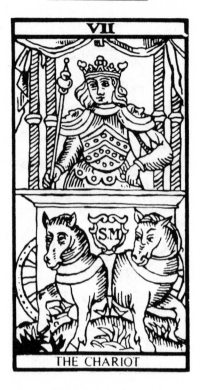

THE CHARIOTEER (GEBURAH-BINAH)

The chariot is a vehicle of motion and in the Kabbalah it is the dynamic counterpart of the throne. The Charioteer is the King in his active role — a strong contract to the merciful and benign ruler who dwells in Chesed. On this path he is empowered to bring down the watery potencies of Binah into archetypal manifestation. He is a mediator, reminding us that we must ourselves become receptors or carriers of light. This is indicated by the central symbolism of the card which depicts the Charioteer either as the all-seeing Eye of God, or the bearer of the Holy Grail. The parallel between *The Charioteer* and the fire-chariot of the Merkabah mystics is of considerable interest, for although many features of this path relate to the element Water, Geburah itself is associated with Mars, and Fire.

THE LOVER

THE LOVERS (TIPHARETH-BINAH)

The twins, whom we first encountered on *The Sun* have now regained their state of original innocence in the Garden of Eden and the Holy Guardian Angel towers above them, bestowing grace. As male and female representations of Tiphareth and Binah we are reminded of the love of the Great Mother Mary for her son, Christ. Greek mythology records a legend showing a similar sort of bond. Castor and Polydeuces (Pollux) were half-brothers, one mortal, the other immortal. In love and compassion, Zeus allowed both of them a common destiny, placing them in the sky as Sun and Moon, thus indicating their complementary solar and lunar attributes. The path of *The Lovers* flows upwards from Tiphareth — the sphere of harmony — and shows the happy and enduring union of opposites.

THE POPE

THE HIEROPHANT (CHESED-CHOKMAH)

This path is that of the 'Triumphant Intelligence'. The paternal, merciful qualities of Chokmah/Chesed are enhanced by the love and grace of Venus who rules this card. We find here an enduring bond of wisdom and mercy: the inspiration of the Spirit manifest as an archetype of enlightened intuition. Divine authority owes its inspirational origin to this region on the Tree and reflects the occult view that a spiritual leader should be an 'initiate' — one who has experienced the illumination of spiritual transcendence.

THE EMPEROR

THE EMPEROR (TIPHARETH-CHOKMAH)

The Emperor faces towards Chokmah, the unmanifested Great Father beyond the Abyss, and for this reason we see him only in profile. The Emperor draws upon the Spirit for his authority and uses it to maintain his universal domain, which lies below him on the Tree of Life. He is paternal, wise and vigilant and, above all, merciful. As the Father of the manifested universe he looks out upon his subjects with compassion, for they owe their being to his union with the Empress.

The Emperor is the peaceful and gentle counterpart of the more aggressive and destructive Charioteer. In Merkabah mysticism the sphere of the Great Father — in particular the Lord of the Throne — was one of the highest spheres of consciousness that could be attained.

THE EMPRESS

THE EMPRESS (BINAH-CHOKMAH)

Here we encroach upon the purest domain of the Tree of Life — the Supernal region above the Abyss. *The Empress*, warm and beneficent, unites Binah and Chokmah — the Great Mother and Father, and symbolically she is the Mother of All Being: from her womb, will flow all the potential images and forms capable of existence in the cosmos.

Mythologically she is Hathor, Rhea, Demeter — in fact all of the archetypal Mother Goddesses have their origin in her. Epitomising love and Nature on a universal scale, she is shown on some Tarot cards sitting among wheat grains and trees, with the River of Life flowing through her fields.

Potentially the path of *The Empress* is the highest expression of balance upon the Tree. Above her lie two paths, one male (*The Magician*) and the other female (*The High Priestess*) which have not yet been counterbalanced by an opposite force. These have only the *potential* for future expression, and *The Fool*, beyond them, symbolises the borderline of manifestation itself. Thus, in *The Empress* we have a very high degree of spiritual illumination indeed: the full integration of both polarities of created forms.

THE HIGH PRIESTESS

THE HIGH PRIESTESS (TIPHARETH-KETHER)

This path, unlike The Empress, reaches to the very peak of Creation in Kether, *The Crown*. Kether, however, is androgynous — transcending sexual polarity — and the High Priestess accordingly has an element of untaintedness about her. As Paul Foster Case has said, if the Empress is Mother Venus (Hathor) then the High Priestess is a transcendental aspect of Diana, the somewhat distant, pristine lunar goddess who has had no sexual contact with a male god and remains an aloof virgin.

The High Priestess has the potential for motherhood, but this occurs lower on the Tree with The Empress — who gives birth to all manifested forms. On the path of *The High Priestess* we are above the Abyss and we approach a virginal, undifferentiated state of being — the all-encompassing unity of *Ain Soph Aur*, the Limitless Light.

THE MAGICIAN

THE MAGICIAN (BINAH-KETHER)

An expression of the Cosmic Intelligence, *The Magician* represents the pure, masculine potency which is as yet unrealised through union with the female polarity. Lying above the Abyss, this path deals with a type of male purity which equates with the virginity of The High Priestess. The Magician stands above Creation in the archetypal sense. However, one hand is raised to bring down the energy of Kether, which is then transmitted further down the Tree.

Mythologically The Magician is Thoth, Logos of the Universe. He embodies the will of the Godhead to manifest: 'In the Beginning was the Word . . .' Thoth is the *divine vibration* which makes creation possible, the personification of the forces of Light which emanate from Kether and are the origin of all manifested forms lower on the Tree.

THE FOOL

THE FOOL (CHOKMAH-KETHER)

The Fool is a symbol for 'he-who-knows-nothing', and upon this path one draws near to the veil of 'No Thing' — that which is unmanifest and beyond the scope of finite existence. Of this realm nothing tangible can be said, for no qualities or attributes may meaningfully be ascribed. The Fool embraces Space and it is his potent energy which in due course descends to the depths of the Kingdom, far below. The Fool precipitates the cosmic process, and the reverberations which follow are like a lightning flash from the mountain-top, coursing from male polarity to female then back to male again, as they zig-zag down the Tree of Life from one *sephirah* to the next. What has previously been unmanifest comes *to be*, and the interplay of force and form produces 'reality' in the world as we know it.

WORKSHOP
THE TAROT
1: MEDITATIONS ON THE MAJOR ARCANA

These Tarot cards represent a rich mythology in symbolic-picture form. However, the most important thing is to allow the cards to 'speak' to you directly by triggering archetypal processes in your mind.

The following meditations are really entry paths to these inner symbols. They have a minimal descriptive content since excessive detail impedes the spontaneous aspects of the mythic encounter.

In all cases the meditations should commence with a progressive relaxation. The facilitator then reads the meditation relaxation aloud, allowing the meditator/s to enter the 'psychic space' of each Tarot card. Impressions should be recorded in a diary.

Appropriate music is listed for each Tarot meditation but you may like to choose alternative music from within the same genre.

The World

We find ourselves in a field of grass. The wind blows gently and we hear birds whistling in the distance.

We feel at peace with Nature. And now, as we watch in our mind's eye, the cycle of her seasons pass before us — the new birth of Spring, the warmth of Summer, the ripeness and wholeness of Autumn. Nature seems barren in Winter but new life will soon return.

We come to a rugged cliff-face and a doorway opens, allowing us to enter. We pass into the rock and find ourselves in a tunnel. A light is shining at the end of the tunnel, and as we draw closer we see that a beautiful naked woman is dancing . . . Her dance is the dance of Nature.

Element: Earth

Appropriate music: 'Grandchester Meadows' from Pink Floyd, *Ummagumma*; 'Ways of Change' from Klaus Schulze, *Blackdance*

Judgement

We have come to a new land. Naked people are all around us, and we are naked too. Suddenly the sky is filled with beautiful music and we lift up our hands to the heavens in praise. We feel the music filling our bodies, giving us energy, vitality, life . . . We rise up into the sky embracing the music, and we know that the gods welcome and protect us.

Element: Air

Appropriate music: 'Why?' from Herbert Joos, *Daybreak*; 'The Great, Great Silence' (opening sequence) from Japetus, *The Great, Great Silence*

The Sun

The Sun is high above us as we come to the foot of a grassy mountain. A large, rocky wall halfway up the slope blocks our path. But we know that we have come to a sacred place and we must be pure in heart and spirit before ascending to the peak. Two children — a boy and a girl — now appear before us. They are young and innocent, and as they begin to dance the light of the Sun pours down upon them. Now we feel the sunlight pouring down on us also, giving us energy and filling us with radiance.

Element: Fire

Appropriate Music: 'Force Majeure' (last third only) from Tangerine Dream, *Force Majeure*

The Moon

We have come to an ocean shore. Waves lap against the beach and, as we watch, a lobster struggles forth onto land. Now two animals parade before us. One is a shaggy wolf, aggressive and hostile. The other is a domestic dog, friendly and protective. This dog leads us up a path towards a rocky outcrop, and as we come closer we see a fortress in the distance. Now we look up into the sky. A beautiful silver crescent Moon fills the heavens. The Moon showers us with a cascade of silver droplets.

Element: Water

Appropriate music: 'Mindphaser' from Klaus Schulze, *Moondawn*

The Star

High above us in the night-sky a bright golden star and a host of silver ones shower the heavens with their light. A crystalline stream flows through this land and kneeling beside the stream is a beautiful, naked woman.

In her hands she holds two flasks, one made of gold, the other of silver. Now, as she lifts her golden flask high into the sky, a stream of liquid light flows from the golden star into her flask. Bending down, she pours this liquid into the stream. Now she comes across to where we are, and our heads become open vessels as she pours the precious water into our bodies. We feel it filling us with energy and life.

Element: Water

Appropriate music: 'Crystal Lake' from Klaus Schulze, *Mirage*

The Tower
We have come to a land which is ominous and strange. An ancient stone tower rises up before us and reaches proudly towards the heavens. But now the sky darkens with storm clouds and we hear a crash of thunder. Suddenly the sky fills with fire and a burst of lightning crashes against the tower. Two proud warriors, and the crumbling battlements of the tower, fall to the ground.
Element: Fire
Appropriate music: 'The Flood' from Lol Creme and Kevin Godley, *Consequences*

The Devil
A gaping hole appears in the ground before us and we enter a subterranean cavern. Strange shadows flicker on the wall as we come before a grotesque creature who stands on a pedestal holding a torch.
His head is like a goat and his legs those of an eagle. Bat wings extend from his back, and an inverted pentagram is visible on his forehead. A man and a woman stand before him, chained to his pedestal like prisoners. At first the figures are threatening but now they seem ludicrous. We smile to ourselves, and as we do so the energy drains out of these strange beings and they dissolve into dust before our eyes.
Element: Earth
Appropriate music: 'Rubycon Part One' from Tangerine Dream, *Rubycon*; 'Nadabrahma' from Rajneesh Foundation musicians, *Nataraj/Nadabrahma*; 'Logos Part One' (first third) from Tangerine Dream, *Logos*

Death
We come now to a gruesome land where the ground is littered with broken human bodies. In the centre of the carnage we see a frenzied skeleton-creature wielding a scythe and taking his human toil. We feel a sense of dread as the skeleton figure comes towards us, but we surrender ourselves to him knowing that our inner spirit will triumph and only our vanities and deceptions will fall upon the ground. Now we feel the limbs of our bodies falling away in fragments and the real essence of our being is flowing forth, freed from constraint. We journey in the spirit vision towards a river and we see that others have come here too. Now we flow with the river and it carries us along. It purifies us, and we sparkle like flashes of light in the stream.
Elements: Earth and Water

Approptiate music: 'Through Metamorphic Rocks' from Tangerine Dream, *Force Majeure*

Temperance
We flow in a crystal river towards the Sun. On the left-hand side of the river it is dark — the very depths of night — while the other shines with the light of new day.
As we flow along the river we come to the land of the Guardian. We see him now, standing astride the river. The Guardian is tall and majestic, his beautiful face ablaze with light. He welcomes us and we have nothing to fear. Beside him, scowling at his feet, is a red lion. The Guardian brings forth a golden flask and bends down to fill it from the stream. Now he pours the waters over the lion and it becomes peaceful. Nearby, a silver eagle whips its wings defiantly in the air. The Guardian brings forth a golden torch and, as we watch, a spark of flame falls down into the eagle's body, filling it with love. Now the Guardian is calling us towards the Sun, and as we draw ever closer we feel the sacred light entering our hearts.
Element: Spirit
Appropriate music: 'Ocean of Tenderness' from Ash Ra, *New Age of Earth*

The Hanged Man
We have come to a place where the air is heavy with water droplets and glistens like shining mist.
We see before us the strange figures of a man hanging upside down, his feet supported by a loop of rope. His coat is decorated with crescent moons and his face is aglow with gentle, lunar light.
Now as we look more closely we see that he is upside down because he is a reflection in water. From high above, rays of light descend into his body and radiate into the mist.
Element: Water
Appropriate music: 'Wind on Water' from Fripp & Eno, *Evening Star*

Justice
We enter a royal chamber and come before a goddess seated on a throne. She has love in her heart but her expression is stern and impartial. In her right hand she holds a large sword and in her left, a set of scales. We submit ouselves before her, lowering our gaze. Now she rests her sword upon our heads, but we feel the power of her mercy flowing over us.
Wonderful music rises up, and fills our entire bodies with vibrant energy.

Element: Fire
Appropriate music: 'Never Let You Go' from Kitaro, *Silver Cloud*

The Wheel of Fortune

We have come to a mighty gateway — doorway to the peak of the mystic mountain. On this gateway is a wheel of light which slowly rotates, sending forth pulsing waves of energy. As the wheel turns, different gods come into view upon its rim. We are journeying towards the very heart of the Cosmos.
Element: Water
Appropriate music: 'Theme Three' from Colosseum, *Valentyne Suite*; 'Dreams Like Yesterday' from Kitaro, *Silver Cloud*

The Hermit

The world grows dark and we find ourselves on the side of a mighty mountain. We feel alone, abandoned, desolate . . . But now a guide appears before us to show us the path of ascent. Our guide is an old man with a long grey beard. He wears a flowing cloak and a hood which partly hides his face. In his right hand he holds a wonderful lantern which glows like a radiant star. He leads us slowly up the mountain path, and as we travel with him we feel our bodies gradually merging together. We become one with him and now the light of his lantern shines from deep within our hearts.
Elements: Earth and Air
Appropriate music: 'Rubycon Part Two' (first third) from Tangerine Dream, *Rubycon*

Strength

We have come to a grassy plain. The sky shines with radiant yellow light. Before us two figures engage in a struggle; one is a beautiful young maiden dressed in a flowing robe, the other a hostile lion. Unafraid of his strength, the maiden opens the jaws of the lion and sings him a soothing song. The song flows down into his heart and lulls him into a state of peace.
Now she places a wreath of white roses around his neck and the lion falls asleep at her feet.
Elements: Fire and Water
Appropriate music: 'Rubycon Part Two' (middle section) from Tangerine Dream, *Rubycon*

The Charioteer

We continue our journey across the grassy plain. The sky has changed colour to a majestic blue and drops of crystal dew hang suspended in the air. Once again we enter a world of mist. Now we hear a sound like thunder. We look upwards to the heavens and see a mighty air-borne chariot drawn by winged horses.

The chariot lands nearby and a tall warrior steps forth. Jewels of light shine from his polished armour as he comes towards us, and he invites us to journey with him through the heavens. We mount his chariot, there is a rumbling of hooves, and we rise up into the sky.

Elements: Air and Water

Appropriate music: 'Bayreuth Return' and 'Wahnfried 1883' from Klaus Schulze, *Timewind*

The Lovers

We come to a sacred grove high upon the mystic mountain. This is the land of innocence and purity, the land of the first man and the first woman. An abundant garden appears before us, and as we watch, a beautiful naked woman and a beautiful naked man embrace in an act of love. Ethereal, haunting music descends from the sky and the garden tingles with dazzling, vibrant colours.

Elements: Earth and Air

Appropriate music: 'Epsilon in Malaysian Pale' from Edgar Froese, *Epsilon in Malaysian Pale*

The Hierophant

As we ascend the mystic mountain we arrive at the Temple of the Sacred Song. Seated before us on a splendid throne is the God of Wisdom. He is awesome to behold. He is the guardian of our secret name. As we bow before him a wonderful song rises up within us and we rejoice.

Elements: Earth and Water

Appropriate music: 'Maroubra Bay' (first half) from Edgar Froese, *Epsilon in Malaysian Pale*

The Emperor

We ascend still higher upon the mystic mountain. Here the land is ablaze with red light. Volcanoes erupt in the distance and the terrain is barren and unfriendly.

We are grateful when, at last, we come to the temple of the Merciful God. He sits upon a red throne, a red cloak flowing from his shoulders to the ground. He is a majestic ruler and we feel at peace with him for we are his children.

But as we rest awhile we sense that he is sad, for his beloved wife is far distant and his kingdom is without a queen.

Elements: Fire and Earth
Appropriate music 'Nowhere — Now Here' (middle section) from Klaus Schulze, *Bodylove*

The Empress

We make our way to a mighty forest where regal, luxuriant trees reach towards the heavens. Passing through the forest we come to an abundant field where golden wheat quivers in the air. A stream of clear, pure water flows through the field and as we trace it to its source we find ourselves before a great goddess seated on her throne. Beautiful flowers decorate her cloak and beams of light dance in her hair.

Now as we watch the goddess, her form seems to dissolve before our eyes and she has become the stream itself. And now the stream has become a river, and the river has become a sea and the sea has become an ocean. And all is still.

Elements: Earth and Water
Appropriate music: 'Origin of Supernatural Probabilities' from Tangerine Dream, *Zeit*

The High Priestess

Beyond the veil of mist, seated on a watery throne, is the Virgin Goddess. We see her dimly through the haze, and as we draw towards her a shimmering silver light floods over us.

The Goddess looks down upon the scroll of memory which rests unfurled upon her knee and once again, uplifted by beautiful and mysterious music, we hear our secret, inner name.

Elements: Water and Spirit
Appropriate music: 'Zeit' from Tangerine Dream, *Zeit*

The Magician

High upon the mystic mountain we come to the Sacred Temple of the Magician. Before us is a mighty doorway, flanked by columns which seem to sustain the universe. Passing into the temple, we come before the great god. His eyes blaze with lightning, thunder roars in his hair, and as he lifts his right arm above his head the air shudders with a vibrant force that fills the temple. Before us we see each of the elements born from a spinning vortex — Earth, Water, Fire, Air. Then, as he passes his hand above them, they dissolve into Spirit.

Elements: Fire, Air and Spirit
Appropriate music: 'Stardancer II' from Klaus Schulze, *Bodylove*

The Fool

Overwhelmed by the awesome nature of our journey, we come at last to the peak of the mystic mountain. Around us, in all directions, infinite space flows into the distance.

We have never been so alone, but as we contemplate that feeling a wonderful sense of love descends upon us. Once again we hear our secret song inside our hearts. And then that song escapes on a gentle breeze and it just wafts away, dispersing its melody in the vastness of space.

And now we are floating . . . floating . . . floating . . .

We see the mountain peak recede in the distance . . . And we are coming home . . .

Element: Spirit

Appropriate music: 'Qasarsphere' from Manuel Gottsching, *Inventions for Electrical Guitar*

2: ADDITIONAL MEDITATIONS

Select music for the card from the Major Arcana which you feel most akin to, and meditate on that card while the music plays.

What are the images and associations that come to mind?

Now meditate on the card you feel most alienated from: this may be a facet of your psyche that you are repressing.

Once again, use music that is appropriate.

THE SIGNS OF THE ZODIAC

Astrology, as we all know, is the study of celestial bodies and their perceived influence on terrestrial events. As a tradition, western astrology has its origins in star-worship and draws primarily on the mythology and culture of ancient Babylonia and Egypt and, to a lesser extent, that of Greece and Rome.

The Babylonians were keen astronomers and identified most of the constellations in the night sky. The Zodiac itself is quite possibly a Babylonian invention and references are made to it in a horoscope dating from 410 BC. The Egyptians, meanwhile, produced the most efficient calendar in the ancient world, dividing the passage of time into a sequence that, substantially, is still in use today. The Egyptian year commenced with the heliacal rising of the star we call Sirius and was divided into 12 months, each of 30 days, with five days added at the end. The Egyptians were also responsible for dividing each day into 24 hours and the vault of the heavens into 36 decans — each the domain of a spirit. While most of the motifs of the Zodiac are originally Babylonian it appears, as we shall see, that others have an Egyptian origin.

The Greeks subsequently drew on Babylonian and Egyptian astrological ideas and developed the concept of the interrelatedness of cosmic patterns and human destiny, producing myths for each of the Zodiac signs except Pisces.[6] Finally, the Roman contribution to astrology as we know it today was to provide us with the names of the Zodiac signs and the planets.

ORIGIN OF THE ZODIAC

The division of the celestial vault into a pattern of constellations reflects the necessarily limited scientific skills of the ancient Babylonian astronomers. Only the brightest stars and planets were visible and we now have a much more extensive knowledge of the planets in our solar system and the stars and galaxies beyond. Modern science has identified nine planets while the Babylonians knew only five, and while traditionally there were only seven stars in the Pleiades of Taurus at least 40 are now known to exist. Similarly, the symbolic patterns of the constellation derived originally from the idea of 'fixed stars' which we now know to be inaccurate because of the phenomenon known as the 'precession of the equinoxes'. Nevertheless the Babylonian achievement was remarkable for its time and Babylonian astronomers were able to predict solar and lunar eclipses with great accuracy.

While the word 'zodiac' has a Greek origin — deriving from *zodiakos* meaning 'a circle of animals' — the signs of the Zodiac are for the most part Babylonian in origin:

Taurus   Taurus was originally Gudanna, the Bull of Heaven. The stars known as the Hyades make a figure like a bull's head, with Aldebaran as one of the eyes. In Babylonian mythology Anu created the Bull of Heaven to kill Gilgamish at the request of Ishtar, after her amorous advances had been rejected by him.

Leo   Known originally as Urgula the Lion, this constellation was also associated by the Akkadians with the Great Dog. Regulus is the brightest point in the constellation and was one of the fixed stars. Known in Babylonia as 'the Lion's Heart', its Roman title means 'little king', and for this reason the sign of Leo has had an ongoing regal connotation.

Virgo   The figure of the Zodiac we know as Virgo is the Roman counterpart of the Greek mother-goddess Demeter. The brightest star in this constellation was known in Babylonia as Spica, the Ear of Corn, and it was one of the fixed stars. Demeter as a goddess of the harvest had an earlier counterpart in the Sumerian grain goddess Nidaba and interestingly this constellation was known to the Babylonians as Absin, the furrow.

Libra   This constellation is located between Spica and Antares. The sign appears to have derived originally from the claws of the Scorpion (an adjacent constellation) and was known in Babylonia as Zabanitu. The month of Teshrit was concerned with fate and destiny and the word 'zabanitu' came to mean 'the scales'.

Scorpio   A spectacular constellation featuring the bright star Antares — the 'Scorpion's Heart' — Scorpio was known as Girtab, and Antares itself was one of the four fixed stars.

Sagittarius   In Babylonia Sagittarius was an Archer rather than a Centaur and the constellation bore the name Pabilsag.

Capricorn   Known in Babylonia as the fish-tailed goat Suhurmashu, or the fish-ram Kusarikku, Capricorn was originally an emblem of Ea, the Babylonian god of water. Capricorn was later classified by Ptolemy as an earth-sign without regard to its mythic origins.

The mythic associations of the following constellations are unclear but they too may have a Babylonian origin:

Gemini   An ostensibly similar constellation was known in Babylon as Mastabbagalgal, 'the Great Twins' and symbolised the close friendship between King Gilgamish and Enkidu. Enkidu originally claimed to be superior to Gilgamish because the goddess Aruru had created him in the image of Anu, ruler of the upper heavens. Gilgamish and Enkidu wrestled each other and thereafter there was no rivalry between them.

Pisces   In the Babylonian Zodiac there was a constellation known as Zibbati, 'The Tails'. However, while this title was associated with the two rivers, the Tigris and Euphrates, it is not known whether the 'tails' were those of fish.

The remaining constellations of the Zodiac, Aries, Cancer and Aquarius, are probably of Egyptian origin:

Aries   There was no ram in the Babylonian Zodiac and it seems certain that the sign of Aries is a tribute to the ram-headed god Amun, who was worshipped at Thebes — the imperial capital during the Middle Kingdom.

Cancer   This constellation may derive from the Egyptian Sign 'Stars of the Water', which was symbolised by the river-turtle. The Greeks later referred to the constellation specifically as the Crab.

Aquarius   Although Ea was the Babylonian god of streams it is more likely that Aquarius derives from Hapi, the god of the Nile River, who was revered because he allowed crops to flourish.

LATER DEVELOPMENTS

The ancient Greeks greatly respected the esoteric knowledge of the Babylonians and adopted several of the Zodiac signs from their cosmology. These included The Maiden, The Twins, The Lion, The Fish, The Scorpion and The Bull. The Archer meanwhile acquired the characteristic of a centaur.

Perhaps the most significant astrological breakthrough, however, was not the interchange of mythological figures but the fact that their symbolic configuration in the sky was found not to be fixed, as the Babylonians had thought. It was the Greek astronomer Hipparchus (c. 194-112 BC) who discovered the phenomenon known as the 'precession of the equinoxes', whereby the points where the ecliptic cuts the equator gradually move westward. Because of this the stars in a specific location gradually change by 50 seconds of arc every year and actually rotate through a vast cycle which has been calculated to take 25,800 years to complete.

Despite this potentially damaging finding, many influential Greek thinkers continued to support the Babylonian concept that the movements of the heavenly bodies were a guide to man's fate on earth, and that the 'exactness' of the cosmic cycles constituted a type of Universal Law. While this type of determinism is unpopular in modern astrology because it undermines the concept of free-will, it became increasingly central to Graeco-Roman astrology, first among the Stoics and then, after the end of the Antonine dynasty, as the official doctrine of Roman emperors. Lucius Septimius Severus, in adopting this philosophy, became the incarnation of the Unconquerable Sun — a cosmic deity on earth — and his law and authority had their foundation in the heavens.

The Egyptian-born astronomer Claudius Ptolemaeus, or Ptolemy (d. 161 AD), had by now systematised astrology in his book *Tetrabiblos* and his categories of favourable and unfavourable aspects in the interpretation of the natal horoscope, the influence of the planets and the idea of physical 'types' associated with each of the signs, had become part of astrological doctrine. They have influenced astrologers ever since.

THE FOUR ELEMENTS AND THE ZODIAC

Ptolemy correlated the signs of the Zodiac with the four elements and also divided the signs into 'cardinal', 'fixed' and 'mutable' as an expression of human nature. According to him:

The *Cardinal Signs*   Aries, Cancer, Libra and Capricorn —

would, 'generally dispose the mind to enter much into political matters, rendering it eager to engage in public and turbulent affairs, fond of distinction, and busy in theology; at the same time ingenious, acute, inquistive, inventive, speculative and studious of astrology and divination'.

The *Fixed Signs* Taurus, Leo, Scorpio and Aquarius — would 'make the mind just, uncompromising, constant, firm of purpose, prudent, patient, industrious, strict, chaste, mindful of injuries, steady in pursuing its object, contentious, desirous of honour, seditious, avaricious and pertinacious'.

The *Mutable Signs* Gemini, Virgo, Sagittarius and Pisces — were 'variable, versatile, not easy to be understood, volatile and unsteady, inclined to duplicity, amorous, wily, fond of music, careless, full of expedients and regretful'.[7]

The Cardinal, Fixed and Mutable signs align with the four elements as follows:

Name	Sign	Element	Nature
Aries	the Ram	Fire	Cardinal
Taurus	the Bull	Earth	Fixed
Gemini	the Twins	Air	Mutable
Cancer	the Crab	Water	Cardinal
Leo	the Lion	Fire	Fixed
Virgo	the Virgin	Earth	Mutable
Libra	the Scales	Air	Cardinal
Scorpio	the Scorpion	Water	Fixed
Sagittarius	the Archer	Fire	Mutable
Capricorn	the Goat	Earth	Cardinal
Aquarius	the Waterbearer	Air	Fixed
Pisces	the Fishes	Water	Mutable

From an astrological point of view *Fire* is symbolic of Divinity and positive force. Fire is characterised as the 'Creator, Sustainer and Destroyer' and these qualities are mirrored in Aries, the first sign of the Zodiac, associated with pioneers and inventive, headstrong individuals; Leo the dignified ruler, under whose sign are born those who are proud and ambitious, and Sagittarius, who personifies the iconoclastic, questing person who cuts through superficialities.

Earth represents the physical world and the practical aspects of life. Taurus the Bull is very much a beast of agriculture and is typical of the stolid 'down to earth' qualities of the sign. Virgo was originally a goddess of the cereal crop and represents the fusion of spirit and matter, while Capricorn symbolises perseverence, dedication and the pursuit of worldly goals.

Air is the domain of thoughts and the mind — the qualities which distinguish man from the animal kingdom. Libra is the cardinal air sign and represents balance, prudence and the ability to bring opposite viewpoints into harmony. Gemini, on the other hand, is 'mutable', or changeable, and people born under this sign are often said to be superficial, with a fickle, unstable nature, despite their powers of imagination. Aquarius inclines to fixed ideas and values self-control and idealism. Aquarians are therefore often intense as well as thoughtful, and may be inclined to be condescending towards the less gifted.

Water is the element which represents the emotions and feelings, and is generally regarded as feminine. Cancer is the most characteristic of the water signs and is romantic, imaginative and sensitive. Scorpio brings the influence of fire to bear, through its ruler Mars, and is characterised by tenacity and determination, where 'feelings are put to the test' and where power may be sought over others. Pisces represents the impressionistic qualities of the element and individuals born under this sign are said to be patient, open to new ideas and sympathetic to others, but often without a positive direction in their own lives.

THE SIGNS AND THEIR RULERS

When we correlate the signs of the Zodiac with their planetary 'rulers' and with their traditional association with different parts of the body, we obtain a much clearer idea of the astrological view of man as a mythic composite. The signs then seem less individual and separate, and more a part of a total process, reflecting the life-rhythms within the human organism as a whole. The correspondences are as follows:

Sign	Part of the Body	Ruler
Aries	Head and face	Mars
Taurus	Throat and neck	Venus
Gemini	Lungs, arms and shoulders	Mercury
Cancer	Breast and stomach	The Moon
Leo	Heart and back	The Sun
Virgo	Intestines and liver	Mercury
Libra	Kidneys	Venus
Scorpio	Genitals	Mars
Sagittarius	Hips and thighs	Jupiter
Capricorn	Knees	Saturn
Aquarius	Ankles, calves and shins	Saturn or Uranus[8]
Pisces	Feet	Jupiter or Neptune[8]

This correlation — read in conjunction with the ascription of the elements detailed above — provides us with an ideal meditative model. Within its own language of symbols, it encompasses man as a whole, in the same way that in the Kabbalah Adam Kadmon incorporates the ten *sephiroth* on the Tree of Life. However the two cosmologies are not interchangeable, and each has its distinctive, unique qualities. A close examination will show that it is not possible to blend these particular systems because, if one were to combine the two, Aries would ideally correlate with *Geburah*, which is associated with the right hand of justice and not with the head. Similarly, Cancer as a watery, lunar sign, would correspond to *Yesod* and not the breast region of *Tiphareth*, and the feet would rest in an earth sign rather than in watery Pisces.

Despite these differences, however, the systems still have their own intrinsic value — as symbolic statements of wholeness. Like the *sephiroth* of the Tree of Life, the signs of the Zodiac provide us with a model of man's inner cosmos and by meditating on the mythic processes involved we transcend the earth realm and enter inner space.

From this viewpoint, the signs of the Zodiac have application not in describing a scientific or 'astronomical' reality so much as portraying a symbolic bond with the universe. The essential message of the ancient astrologers was that man has a link with Creation. Its universal processes are reflected most profoundly in man's inner being.

WORKSHOP

THE SIGNS OF THE ZODIAC

1: THE BASIC VISUALISATION

This is essentially a familiarisation exercise designed to give the signs of the Zodiac an inner, experiential quality. First prepare a compilation tape which includes three identical music sequences for Fire (1 minute); Earth (1 minute), Air (1 minute) and Water (1 minute) — 12 minutes in total. They should be in this sequence because, commencing with Aries, the signs of the Zodiac follow this progression in the calendar cycle. Ensure when you prepare your tape that one element merges into the next.

Sit in a comfortable position in a darkened room and work through the progressive relaxation exercise described earlier (see Workshop, Chapter One). As the music plays three times through the four elements in turn, visualise each Zodiac sign emerging from the element associated with it. It is helpful to imagine the Zodiac figure actually being formed from the element, so that Virgo has a body of earth, Leo is a lion of fire, Pisces are translucent fishes which appear from the watery depths, and so on.

Note: It may be helpful at first if the workshop leader announces to the meditator/s at one minute intervals: 'We are now visualising the Fire-Ram of Aries', 'We are now visualising the Earth-Bull of Taurus' . . . through the whole cycle.

2: THE CROSS OF BALANCE

Using the same compilation tape, identify your own sun sign and also the three other signs of the Zodiac which complete your personal 'Cross of Balance'. These are as follows:

The Cardinal Cross:
Aries (Fire); Capricorn (Earth); Libra (Air); Cancer (Water)
The Fixed Cross:
Leo (Fire); Taurus (Earth); Aquarius (Air); Scorpio (Water)
The Mutable Cross:
Sagittarius (Fire); Virgo (Earth); Gemini (Air); Pisces (Water)

The effect of the following visualisation is to extend the range of personal qualities expressed in the sun sign by drawing into consciousness the three complementary signs.

If you are working singly you can start the meditation with music for your own sun sign but if you are in a group situation you will have to wait for the music to play through the elements until your own sign is reached as a point of commencement. The music will play through your sequence twice in a complete cycle, and three times if your sun sign is associated with Fire.

As before, visualise the signs of the Zodiac emerging from their elements but remember that the sequence this time is purely through the signs which make up your Cross of Balance, and not through the Zodiac as a whole. When you have finished the visualisation, withdraw your focused attention and relax until the music finishes.

3: THE GOLDEN DAWN ASTROLOGY VISUALISATION

The following correlation between the signs of the Zodiac and the notes of the chromatic scale was proposed by a leading member of the Hermetic Order of the Golden Dawn, Allan Bennett (Frater Iehi Aour), who was a major influence on Aleister Crowley. Bennett also matched the notes to colours of the spectrum, and these are quite different from the elemental ascriptions. For example, Sagittarius, a Fire sign, is correlated with the colour blue, and Cancer, a Water sign, with amber (yellow/orange):

Zodiac Sign	Musical Note	Colour
Aries	C	Red
Taurus	C#	Red-Orange
Gemini	D	Orange
Cancer	D#	Amber
Leo	E	Yellow
Virgo	F	Green-Yellow
Libra	F#	Green
Scorpio	G	Blue-Green
Sagittarius	G#	Blue
Capricorn	A	Indigo
Aquarius	A#	Violet
Pisces	B	Magenta

For the workshop it is ideal to use either a synthesiser or an electric piano with vibrator so that the resonance of the notes can be extended.

The session is held in a darkened room. The Meditator/s sit comfortably, relax and close their eyes.

The musician serves as a facilitator and plays through the chromatic scale, allowing each note to linger for a time in the air. The facilitator also says: 'This is the note C for Aries . . . visualise red . . .'; 'This is the note C# for Taurus . . . visualise red-orange . . .' and so on. Each note should be spaced apart so that it is distinct from the next.

Meditator/s: As the notes are played in sequence, try to recall: which combinations of the Zodiac signs, musical notes and colours worked especially well for you? Which ones seemed inappropriate? Did any associated images arise?

The cycle can be played through several times to allow specific impressions to be confirmed. Finish with a group discussion: is the correlation valid? Does it have value for personal growth?

4: ADVANCED MEDITATION

Preparation: Use the same compilation music that you selected for the Basic Visualisation and add a sequence of Spirit music at the front and end.

Facilitator: While the Spirit music sequence is playing, lead the meditator/s through a progressive relaxation: ask all participants to stand with their legs together, and their eyes closed. They should eliminate tension in their bodies by slowing the breath. When you recognise that the Fire music is about to commence, lead the group through the following procedure and ensure that, with each Zodiac sign visualised in the body, you are co-ordinating the music with the imagery:

'Now we will visualise each sign of the Zodiac coming to life inside us, and shining like a beacon. First imagine an intense white light just above your head. It is pure, radiant light, and it is entering your head now, and passing down into your body. Feel this light illuminating your face. Vibrate a personal image of Fire coming forth from the white light and visualise Aries the Ram occupying this part of your body.

Now bring the white light down to your neck and vibrate an image of Earth. Imagine the robust figure of Taurus the Bull residing in this part of your body.

Now bring the white light down still further and imagine it spreading across each of your shoulders and down both arms, and down into your lungs also. I'd like you to vibrate the image of Air, feel it enlivening your body, and imagine that Gemini the Twins reside here — one in each arm.

Now bring the white light down into your chest and extend it so that it radiates into your stomach. Vibrate an image of soothing, refreshing Water and visualise Cancer the Crab ruling this part of your body.

Now focus the white light in your heart and radiate it around to your back. Vibrate an image of Fire and visualise Leo the Lion residing here.

Now bring the white light down into your intestines and into your liver. Feel the white light filling and sustaining them and vibrate an image of Earth. Visualise Virgo the Maiden residing in these organs of your body.

Now move the white light in a stream across to your kidneys and vibrate them with Air. This is the location of Libra the Scales.

Now bring the white light down to your genitals — the seat of life. Vibrate an image of Water and visualise Scorpio the Scorpion residing in this part of your body.

Now I'd like you to bring the white light down even further into your body. Radiate it into your hips and into your thighs. Vibrate an image of Fire and visualise Sagittarius the Centaur, with his bow and arrow, residing here.

And now I'd like you to imagine the white light moving down even further so that it reaches your knees. Vibrate an image of Earth in both of your knees and visualise Capricorn the Sea-Goat residing here.

And now bring the white light down into your calves, and down into your shins, and down into your ankles. I'd like you to vibrate an image of Air, enlivening these parts of your body and visualise Aquarius with his flask residing here.

Now you feel the white light reaching your feet. You feel the light extending into each of your toes, and into your heels, and into the soles of your feet. Vibrate an image of Water, and visualise Pisces the Fishes residing in each of your feet.

(short pause: commence Space music)

Now I'd like you just to reflect for a moment on how you have brought this whole cosmos of the Zodiac to life in your body . . .

Reaffirm the feeling that white light has passed from the crown of your head down to your feet and feel that you now reach from earth way up to the heavens. You feel huge, without limits. You are part of the Cosmos.

(short pause)

Now I would like you to imagine the white light, which is down in your feet, retracing its course up through the centre of your body. Think of it like a liquid stream of energy and raise it slowly from your feet, up through your thighs, your abdomen, your chest and your neck until once again it is focused in your head.

Now I would like you to stand with your legs apart. Keep your eyes closed and extend your arms out horizontally on each side as you face ahead. We are now standing in the shape of the Human Pentagram.

Still focusing the white light in your head, I'd like you now to imagine it streaming clockwise in a circle so that you can see it in your mind's eye, moving in an arc around to your right hand. And now the white light continues in an arc down to your right foot. Now it passes from your right foot across to your left foot, and now it begins to climb in an arc of radiance towards your left hand. And now the light continues on its path and comes back up to your head, completing the Circle of Radiance.

And you stand within it, affirming the whole circle of white light, feeling it pulse around you, and you radiate the love of the Universe.

And just think this thought to yourself:

The Cosmos is within me: the Cosmos and I are One

The Cosmos is within me: the Cosmos and I are One

The Cosmos is within me; the Cosmos and I are One

And now, if you would like to lie down on a cushion or rest in a chair to reflect quietly on that, please feel free to do so . . .'

(conclude with group discussion)

THE EGYPTIAN BOOK OF THE DEAD

The death and rebirth cycles found in different world mythologies provide an excellent framework for personal growth because they invariably describe states of transformation which may be related symbolically to the development of human consciousness. Among the religions of ancient western civilisations one of the finest examples of a rebirth cycle is found among the so-called Egyptian 'Books of the Dead', specifically in a work known as the *Book of the Am-Tuat*. This is not the most familiar of the Egyptian funerary texts: Sir Wallis Budge's translation of the *Theban Recension of the Book of the Dead* — a collection of hymns and religious texts known simply as *The Book of the Dead* — is the most famous of these works, and there is also an Osirian text titled *The Book of Gates*. However, for the purpose of guided imagery and meditation a complete and relatively simplified cycle is ideal; the *Am-Tuat* has been selected here because it emphasises the cyclic death and rebirth of the Sun-god and provides us with inspired images relating to Ra's encounter with, and conquest over, the powers of darkness.

For the meditator the journey of consciousness through the Egyptian underworld becomes an awesome exploration of the forces of life and death — a profound rite of passage. The ancient Egyptian who placed his destiny at the mercy of the Sun-god hoped to be chosen to journey with him in the sacred barque, conquering the forces of the night and participating in the triumph of the Sun-god as he emerged with the new dawn. Here in the never-ending daily cycle of the Sun's passage across the sky was a profound assurance that the forces of light would forever prove victorious over evil and darkness.

The aim of all Egyptian Books of the Dead, as Budge points out, was to provide 'a description of the regions through which their souls would have to pass on their way to the Kingdom of Osiris, or to that portion of the sky where the sun rose, and which would supply them with the words of power and magical names necessary for making an unimpeded journey from this world to the abode of the blessed'.[9] Although for the ancient Egyptians such texts related to the post-mortem state we can make use of these descriptions as esoteric maps of consciousness. All major magical initiations are, in themselves, a type of death and renewal process — invariably involving the transition from old perceptions to new. In addition, there are clear parallels between the shaman's journey in an altered state of consciousness and what we know of the death experience.

What is so interesting about the *Book of the Am-Tuat* is that the journey of the deceased through the dungeons of the underworld mirrors life in the real world: the dragons and serpents encountered as obstacles in the Tuat, or nether regions, are exaggerated versions of the real snakes and crocodiles that presented a threat to everyday existence in ancient Egypt. Similarly, the Sun-god provided sustenance in the halls of the Tuat in the same way that the sun allowed crops to thrive in the physical world. In addition, Ra's mythic journey through the underworld was based on actual localities in Egypt: sometimes he would pass along a mighty river, at other times across sand-dunes and desert regions. From all of these aspects we form an impression that perhaps the after-death realm is an altered state of consciousness populated with the images of waking consciousness, enlarged and embellished by the imagination. Whether this is true or not, there is no doubt that the Egyptian after-life reflected the familar patterns of life on earth. The daily triumph of the Sun-god over the hours of night was taken as a guarantee of the possibility of eternal life — an assurance that all virtuous and righteous 'followers of the light' would live on after death and, like Ra in his transformations, conquer every possible foe — from the fire-breathing serpents in the underworld dungeons through to the mighty dragon Apophis.

THE EGYPTIAN CONCEPT OF THE OTHER WORLD

The Egyptians observed the passage of the sun across the sky each day and its consequent setting in the west, and formed the belief that the night-land was the abode of the dead. During the twelve hours of darkness Ra journeyed that land, bringing light, life and sustenance to all those who lived there.

However, there are some paradoxical elements in ancient Egyptian religious belief because the stars in the heavens were regarded by many as spirits of the dead and obviously those who had now joined the company of the gods were way beyond the earth. A Pyramid Text contains the following passage: '. . . he goes to heaven like the hawks and his feathers are like those of the geese, he rushes to heaven like a grasshopper. Thus he flies away from you, ye men; he is no more upon earth . . . He ascends to heaven, to thee, of Ra, with the head of a falcon and the wings of a goose . . . in the night he is born; he belongs to those who are behind Ra, to those who are before the morning star.[10]

Despite this belief, for the Egyptians of the New Kingdom (1580-1370 BC), when the Books of the Dead were compiled and transcribed upon papyrus, the Tuat was believed to exist below the earth. The dead became known as the 'dwellers in the west' and entry to the other world was through Manu, the Mountain of the Sunset — which lay on the west bank of the Nile.

In yet another sense the Tuat was also on the plane of earth itself — a counterpart of Upper and Lower Egypt in which the twelve hours of darkness corresponded to different regions of the kingdom. For example, in the *Am-Tuat* the first division beyond the entry chamber corresponded to Abydos, and there were subsequent divisions which related to the desert regions around Memphis ruled by Seker, the delta districts of Busiris and Mendes ruled by Osiris and the city of Heliopolis ruled by Annu (Temu-Khepera-Ra).

The deceased person, in mummified form, entered the Tuat in a boat and for the most part journeyed with Ra along a mighty river. However in some parts of the Tuat the river disappeared altogether and the journey was across treacherous snake-ridden deserts: it finally culminated, as we shall see, with passage through the body of a giant serpent!

Osiris, in his role as Lord of the Dead, was widely considered to be the archetype for all deceased souls, and sections of the Tuat were ruled by him. Indeed, some of the dead earned the right — through their purity and good deeds on earth — to live in his kingdom. Here they were nourished by barley cakes, bread and beer, and worked the Field of Earu in the same way that they had tilled the pastures of the Nile during their lives on earth. Other deceased souls spent eternity traversing the heavens with Ra, welcomed by the gods and, according to the texts, regarded as their equals.[11]

Of course, the various Books of the Dead also describe the grim fate that was likely to befall the impure and wicked, and the Tuat was no place to be cast aside. As Budge succinctly writes 'In all the Books of the Other World we find pits of fire, abysses of darkness, murderous knives, streams of boiling water, foul stenches, fiery serpents, hideous animal-headed monsters and creatures, and cruel, death-dealing beings of various shapes . . .'[12]

However, it is precisely because of the marked contrasts in after-death imagery — the clear distinction at all times between darkness and light — that the books of the Tuat are so distinctive as rites of passage and, in turn, as a basis for guided visualisation. In addition, as mentioned in an earlier chapter, the power of sound was vitally important, and Ra conquered his foes in the darkness through magical utterances known as *hekau*. According to Egyptian cosmology, sound had brought all manifested forms into existence in the first place and now here in the Other World, Ra was revivifying the world of departed spirits with his powerful rebirth energies of light and sound.

BACKGROUND ON THE TEXT

The *Book of Am-Tuat* was compiled by the priests of Amen-Ra at

Thebes. Their purpose was to demonstrate the supremacy of their god over all of the other deities, including Osiris, and to encompass in one cycle all the principal regions of Egypt. Each of these districts — Abydos, Memphis, Mendes, Heliopolis — was considered to have its own underworld, but in the Theban *Am-Tuat* these were drawn into a whole, linked through the Sun-god's travail. As Ra set off on his journey he would visit each division of the Tuat in turn, issuing commands to the gods of the regions and having as his special guide a goddess assigned to that particular hour of the night. Ra was considered, on this journey, to be a corpse and was depicted with the head of a ram. The rite of passage through the Tuat in fact transformed the solar deity from Afu-Ra (the dead Sun-god) to Khepera (god of the new morning) and this process of life, death and renewal continued for all eternity.

The dead person, or disembodied spirit, joined Ra's procession through the Tuat after appropriate funerary rites and offerings had been made by relatives and after magical amulets had been placed on the mummified body. The following is a summary of the divisions of the Other World presented in the *Am-Tuat* from the viewpoint of the deceased and, as will be seen, the journey presents a profound process of transformation. From a meditative point of view it is appropriate to view the sequence as an encounter with the dark forces of the psyche (the 'underworld' or unconscious) and the gradual triumph of light and harmony (spiritual rebirth).

Division One: The Western Antechamber

Evening has come and the Sun-god enters the western vestibule of the Tuat, filling it with light. However, before entering the main section of the Tuat — which really begins in Division Two — Afu-Ra must travel for 120 leagues along the River Urnes until encountering the first of the underworld deities. The barque contains the body of the dead Sun-god, together with a crew of seven gods and one goddess — all aspects of himself. Nearby a smaller boat carries the beetle Kheper-en Asar, thereby demonstrating that the transformation of the Sun-god has already begun.

Songs of praise rise up as Afu-Ra's self-propelled barque moves along. The Sun-god uses his magical words of power and is allowed to proceed.

Division Two: the Kingdom of Khenti-Amenti-Osiris

Khenti-Amenti-Osiris was the Lord of the Other World at Abydos. In this region of the Tuat the River Urnes is 309 leagues long and 120 leagues wide. Isis, the mother goddess and wife of Osiris, and her sister Nephthys, join the barque in the form of uraei (sacred serpents personifying the power of the Pharoah). Four boats move ahead of Afu-Ra: the first carries the Full Moon and the other symbols of the harvest and of Lord Osiris himself. Afu-Ra and Osiris combine to battle against Apophis (Apep) and his serpent allies, and Afu-Ra then enters a region known as the 'Field of the Gods of Grain' where he is able to rest. Six grain gods stand to the right of the barque and six gods holding a phallus-knife (symbolic of fertility) to the left. The grain gods offer nourishment to the followers of the Sun-god but this has no effect until Afu-Ra himself utters words of power to sustain them all.

Division Three: the Kingdom of Khenti-Amenti-Osiris
Steered by a hawk-headed god, the barque of Afu-Ra now enters the region of the 'Secret Souls'. The River Urnes is of a similar length and width as before, and the region is an extension of the kingdom of Osiris which we entered in Division Two. Three boats precede the barque of Afu-Ra and they contain hawk gods and mummified deities symbolic of Osiris. Afu-Ra calls to Osiris as he approaches the throne of his ally. His words bring to life many lesser deities — minor forms of Osiris — and the souls of the wicked are consumed in fire. Songs of praise rise up and Afu-Ra is acknowledged as the supreme master of the Tuat.

Division Four: the Kingdom of Seker
We come now to a kingdom of dark, barren deserts where multi-headed serpents roam about causing havoc. The ruler of this domain is Seker, a hawk-headed god who, for the inhabitants of Memphis personified decay. It is so murky in this division of the Tuat that Seker himself is not visible. There is no river here and Afu-Ra is forced to leave his barque and to travel by land. His new vehicle is shaped like a two-headed serpent and it glides across the sand, drawn by four gods and emitting rays of light. Afu-Ra calls forth into the darkness and moves forward cautiously with his retinue.

Division Five: the Kingdom of Seker
This division of the Tuat contains secret passage-ways leading to Seker's hidden chambers but the dark god lives deep beneath a mound of sand and is protected by two man-headed sphinxes. A huge pyramid covers Seker's domain guarded by a goddess known as 'the protector of the apex'. As the Sun-god draws near he seeks the guidance of the beetle Khepera to ensure safe passage, and he in turn begins the process of revivifying the dead god. A huge noise erupts from the earth as Afu-Ra passes by.

The dangers of the Kingdom of Seker include two serpents — Ankhaapau who dwells in billowing fire and Tepan, who resides near a lake of boiling water. However, the entourage of Afu-Ra passes through Seker's domain safely by journeying above his subterranean chamber rather than by seeking to penetrate the darkness beneath the pyramid.

Division Six: the Kingdom of Osiris

Once again there is a river along which to travel, so Afu-Ra discards his serpent-vehicle for a boat drawn by paddles. This division is characterised by a series of close-set chambers which contain various forms of Osiris, and it is also a place where the spirits of the blessed reside.

Afu-Ra now rests upon the back of a five-headed serpent and draws the beetle Khepera, symbolic of rebirth, towards him. Afu-Ra has reached the half-way point in the Tuat and from now on will be travelling steadily towards the Mountain of the Sunrise. Among the many gods surrounding him is a monstrous serpent called Am-Khu who 'eats the spirits' of the enemies of the Sun-god. The Four Children of Horus spring to life from the back of this serpent when they hear the voice of Afu-Ra.

Division Seven: the Kingdom of Osiris

From now on Afu-Ra may be regarded as a form of Khepera. Isis has rejoined the barque and Afu-Ra is protected by a serpent called Mehen whose body forms a canopy above his head. The river is shallow here and the boat has to be towed. There are potential dangers from crocodiles and snakes, and especially from the serpent-monster Apophis (also called Neha-Hra) who sprawls across a sand-bank.

Isis uses her magical words of power to protect the boat and two other gods manage to wound Apophis by fixing him to the ground with six huge knives.

Afu-Ra now enters a region where there are four rectangular buildings, each containing the head of a man. The buildings are tombs and the four heads represent the Sun-god who is returning to life. Horus and the twelve gods and goddesses of the hours assist the solar deity on his journey.

Finally the barque passes beside a great crocodile who lies full-length over the tomb of Osiris. Afu-Ra calls to Osiris, who raises his head in acknowledgement as the procession moves by.

Division Eight: the Kingdom of Osiris

Once again, a group of deities tows the barque of Afu-Ra. Isis, meanwhile, has departed — indicating that there are fewer dangers to encounter in this division of the Tuat. Four crowned rams lead the procession: the first with a solar disc between its horns, the second wearing the crown of Southern Egypt, the third wearing the crown of the North and the fourth a solar disc and plumes.

Afu-Ra passes a group of mummified gods who respond with a murmering like 'the hum of many honey-bees'.

Division Nine: the Kingdom of Osiris

In this division the boat of the Sun-god moves without towing. Twelve sailors paddle with both hands and sing praises to Afu-Ra. As they do so, they also scatter water on the spirit-inhabitants of the region.

Twelve protective uraei on the right-hand side of Afu-Ra lighten the darkness with fire which pours from their mouths; other deities provide food for the gods as the barque journeys through. To the left of Afu-Ra are twelve gods and twelve goddesses: the gods are avengers of Osiris and do battle with his enemies while the goddesses, uplifted by the sound of the great god's voice, sing his praises.

Division Ten: the Kingdom of Temu-Khepera-Ra

Afu-Ra now travels through a region of the Tuat which corresponds to the kingdom at Heliopolis. It is in this division that the germ of new life enters the body of the dead Sun-god and revivifies him, so he may eventually emerge from the Tuat in splendour and glory.

The barque of Afu-Ra is neither rowed nor towed, but moves by itself. A serpent with a black hawk on its back precedes it, and goddesses of the North and South stand nearby. They are followed by another serpent and a group of twelve gods. Of the latter, four carry arrows and have discs for heads, four carry javelins and four carry bows — these beings are protectors of Afu-Ra against his enemies.

To the right of the barque are twelve lakes of water and there are figures in the water who pose a potential threat to the passage of the barque. However, Horus stands nearby encouraging them to enjoy the health and prosperity available to all allies of Afu-Ra.

The beetle Kheper-Ankh can be seen pushing a ball of sand as he moves along and nearby stands the Ape god Af-ermen-Maat-f who holds the Eye of Horus and sings praises to it.

Division Eleven: the Kingdom of Temu-Khepera-Ra

We now draw towards the Mountain of the Sunrise in preparation for the rebirth of the Sun-god. The boat is drawn by twelve deities who have attached the serpent Mehen to the craft and are using his body as a rope. Various gods come forth as Afu-Ra passes, some wearing the Red Crown and some the White. To the left of the Sun-god's boat Horus presides over pits of fire into which are thrown the enemies of Ra.

Division Twelve: the Eastern Antechamber
Like Division One, the twelfth hour of Afu-Ra's journey is not strictly within the Tuat but is a transitionary chamber adjoining it. We now enter the womb of the sky-goddess Nut, who will in turn give birth to the Sun-god — allowing him to come forth into the world of light.

To effect the rebirth, the beetle Khepera leads the boat, and twelve servants of Ra, into the tail of a huge serpent, Ankh-Neteru. In due course the boat will emerge from the serpent's mouth but during the passage through its body Afu-Ra transforms into Khepera. The twelve servants similarly come forth as 'rejuvenated forms of Ra'.

As Khepera emerges from the thighs of Nut twelve goddesses tow the boat of the new-born god into the sky. 'They bring with them the soft wind and breezes which accompany the dawn and guide the god to Shu' — personification of the earth's atmosphere. Thus Khepera begins his journey across the sky . . .

As we can see from this summary, the Egyptian underworld was a region of torments and dangers but also provided bountiful rewards for those who had earned them. An inspiring tribute to the power of light and the supremacy of the 'sacred vibration' — the voice of the Sun-god — the *Book of Am-Tuat* presents a remarkable rite of passage. As a universal journey of renewal, it provides a wonderful framework for guided visualisation.

WORKSHOP

THE EGYPTIAN BOOK OF THE DEAD

GUIDED IMAGERY VISUALISATION FOR THE JOURNEY THROUGH THE TUAT

Preparation: Make a compilation tape of appropriate music for each of the sequences described below in the guided meditation (see listing at conclusion)

Facilitator: Read the following text to the meditator/s in conjunction with the selected music. Meditator/s should lie relaxed on the floor in near total darkness, with their eyes closed. The workshop should begin with a progressive relaxation (as for Workshop, Chapter One)

I

'I would like you to imagine that you are now about to undertake a journey of spiritual rebirth through the different regions of the Egyptian underworld. The important thing to remember is that you are taking the role of the Sun-god and this means you will be bringing your light and radiance to the dark regions of the Tuat. You will notice that as you shine your light forth, any menacing images will recede before you, retreating as you pass by. Remember at all times that *you* are the dominant force in the Tuat — you are the Sun itself — and this is *your* journey of self-transformation.

Now, as you lie relaxed, I would like you to imagine that, like a mummy, you are protected by embalming bandages. Imagine them first looped around your feet and now imagine that they encircle your body — all the way up your legs and your arms and your chest, to your chin: leaving your head uncovered. Accustom yourself to this feeling and sense the protective, armouring quality which the bandages provide. And now focus your consciousness in your head. I'd like you to imagine that your head is filled with luminous, spiritual radiance so that you are rather like a beacon sending your rays of light in all directions . . .

II

And now feel that you are travelling on a boat which is drawn along by other gods who surround and protect you, and that this boat is passing down into the earth along a mighty river. It is a vast and awesome river that stretches before you, but you are its master, and as the boat moves serenely in the waters the darkness fills with the light you send forth.

Imagine also, as you move along, that a wonderful song is coming forth from your heart, and that this is the Song of Life which sustains all positive forms within the Tuat.

Now, as you journey further, you come to the Field of the Gods of

Grain and you are given nourishment — fresh food from the golden fields — to sustain you on your journey. And still you continue and as you go further into the Tuat you hear songs of praise rise up in your honour.

But now the Tuat grows somewhat darker and you have to focus your light more intently. The ancient hawk-god Seker lives here, deep beneath the earth, and the river has dried up. So instead you move across the desert sands, above Seker's domain. Now there are rumblings in the earth beneath you, but you pass above these rumblings without a care, hurling beams of light upon the sand as you do so. And now on your left-hand side you see a huge snake, looped and coiled in flames. But as you cast your gaze upon him he grows smaller and smaller and is finally consumed in his own fire.

Meanwhile, on your right-hand side another huge snake rises up — this time from a pool of boiling water. Now, as you turn your gaze upon him you send forth a beam of light and this evaporates the water and dissolves his form like steam wafting in the air.

III

So now you go forward even further in the Tuat and you begin to feel that like the reborn Osiris a new vitality is entering your body. And from now on that feeling of inner light will slowly intensify as you travel through the Tuat.

Still you venture along the river, and as you do so various welcoming images pass before your eyes. As you offer light to them, songs of praise rise up. And now you notice that twelve serpents of fire have formed a protective circle around you as you move forward, and the boat proceeds still further through the Tuat.

The light is welling up within you as you move steadily towards the Mountain of the Sunrise.

Now, the entry through this mountain is strange indeed because you are about to pass through a long tunnel, and that tunnel is the body of the giant serpent Mehen. But you have nothing to fear and now you are entering his tail, drawn by the protector gods that lead your boat. As you move through his body in stages the light builds up within your body. And you feel your mummy-bandages falling away, and it is as if you have a new, beautiful, radiant body, which, in its innocence and purity, is about to come forth into the world.

Now as you prepare to emerge from the snake tunnel you hear your mother, the sky goddess, calling to you to be born.

And ever so gradually you feel you are coming forth from her thighs, and there is a wonderful feeling of release, a serene and wonderful feeling of release. You are coming through . . . you are being born . . . and it is beautiful.

And you are floating free, floating into the sky. And as you float still higher into the heavens a wonderful radiance shines from your body, for you are illuminating the world with your purity and love . . .'

(pause)

'Now I'd like you to just stay with that wonderful feeling of peace and innocence and light, and simply relax . . . relax and dwell in the beauty of it all'.

(After allowing a period for relaxation the facilitator may like to gradually lead the group back to an awareness of the familiar world, and the meditators can relate their experiences)

Appropriate music;

Sequence I: 'Above Chiangmai'/'An Arc of Doves' from Brian Eno and Harold Budd, *The Plateaux of Mirror*

Sequence II: 'Nowhere — now here' from Klaus Schulze, *Bodylove* (first half)

Sequence III: 'Ocean of Tenderness' from Ash Ra, *New Age of Earth*

KUNDALINI YOGA

Kundalini Yoga is a form of Tantra in which, according to practitioners, the latent *Shakti* energy within one's being is awakened and raised through the different *chakras* of the body. As a method of expanding consciousness it encompasses many specific techniques, among them the use of mantras, visualisation, development of the five senses and breath control. It also includes deities from Indian mythology (who are ascribed to the *chakras*), symbolic animals (which characterise different aspects of mystical consciousness) and the Tattva motifs of the five elements: Earth, Water, Fire, Air and Spirit.

Kundalini Yoga presents the essential aim of yoga perhaps more clearly than other of the related spiritual paths. The very word 'yoga' itself comes from the Sanskrit *Yuj*, meaning 'to yoke' and the aim of yoga is union — with the Higher Self, the Godhead, Brahman. In Kundalini Yoga this union is expressed as the merging of two opposites — Shiva and Shakti, who represent the male and female polarities of existence respectively. While the Higher Self (*Atman*) is represented as male, all created forms, all manifestations of life energy, intelligence, will, thoughts and feelings are considered to be female, and aspects of Shakti. As the Great Goddess she encompasses the three *gunas*, or characteristics of creation, known as *sattva* (purity), *rajas* (activity) and *tamas* (inertia) as well as the five elements from which the universe is formed. As Swami Sivananda Sarasvati lucidly expresses it, 'She is the primal force of life that underlies all existencies. She vitalises the body through her energy. She is the energy in the Sun, the fragrance in the flowers, the beauty in the landscape . . . the whole world is her body. Mountains are her bones. Rivers are her veins. Ocean is her bladder. Sun and Moon are her eyes. Wind is her breath. *Agni* is her mouth . . .'[13]

Beyond manifestation is the transcendental domain of Lord Shiva, and the task in Kundalini Yoga is to arouse the energy of the Goddess so she may be once again united with him in the Supreme Bliss of *Samadhi*.

Kundalini Yoga clearly identifies in man a potentially cosmic process. The gods are within — the purpose is to bring them to life, to unleash their energy. There are numerous energy channels in the body — according to some yogic sources, as many as 350,000 — but the principal one in Kundalini Yoga is the path which the *Shakti* energy should take in passing through the *chakras* to the crown of the head. This is the *Sushumna*, the *nadi* (or energy channel) which corresponds to the central nervous system of the body. Around it are coiled two other major channels, *Pingala* — which is masculine and associated with the heat of the Sun — and *Ida* — which is feminine and is represented by the cool, reflected light of the Moon. *Ida* and *Pingala* meet in the lowest of the *chakra* energy centres in the body, known as *Muladhara*, and again in the sixth centre known as *Ajna*. The essential purpose in arousing energy from the base *chakra* is to lift *Shakti* from the 'gross' levels of physical existence to the pure and transcendent level represented by *Sahasrara*, the highest *chakra* in the body. In so doing, the practitioner's awareness of the universe and its energies gains new meaning, for *Shakti* 'leads the individual from *chakra* to *chakra*, from plane to plane, and unites him with Lord Shiva'.

So Kundalini Yoga is essentially about energy, and that is reflected in the use of mantras (energy as sound) and in the visualisation of specific colours (energy as light). It is also demonstrated by the dance of Shiva and Shakti as they unite one with the other dissolving old forms and creating the universe anew (energy as movement). The *chakras* are themselves sources of subtle energy depicted as 'wheels' (the literal meaning of the word) or as 'lotuses' (*padma*). In some Kundalini tracts it is said that the petals of the lotus droop downwards until the *Shakti* energy is aroused to bring them to life, and the *Sushumna* thus becomes a conduit for powerful spiritual energies as each *chakra* is progressively transcended. As yogic practitioner Madhav Pandit explains, the process involves flowing from one *chakra* to the next by visualising each Tattva in turn, dissolving it in the associated mantra vibration, and then merging it with the next Tattva in sequence. The five elements — Earth, Water, Fire, Air and Spirit — which are associated with the first five *chakras*, are in due course integrated and then — in an act of transcedence — Shakti is united with her consort in the sixth sphere. *Ajna*. The seventh *chakra*, *Sahasrana*, lies beyond the realms of human consciousness and as Carl Jung has written, is 'a philosophical concept with no substance whatever for us — it is beyond any possible experience'.[14]

THE CHAKRA SYSTEM OF KUNDALINI YOGA

Some western interpreters of Kundalini Yoga have identified the *chakras* with specific nerve plexuses, ganglia and glands in the body. However yoga authority Haridas Chaudhuri notes in his article 'Yoga Psychology' that this is misleading and contrary to Tantric teaching. Chaudhuri describes the *chakras* as 'consciousness potentials' which only assume meaning as the Kundalini is aroused. The *chakras* themselves lie within the *Brahmanadi* — the innermost channel within the *Sushumna*. While there is a *correlation* between the *chakras* and various parts of the body the chakras do not *equate* with them. The 'locations' are nevertheless necessary for visualisation purposes so the *chakras* may be summarised as follows:

First chakra *Muladhara* at the base of the spine, near the coccyx (associated with the pelvic plexus, testes and ovaries)

Second chakra *Svadisthana* two inches below the navel in the sacral region (associated with the hypogastric plexus and adrenal glands)

Third chakra *Manipura* three inches above the navel in the lumbar region (associated with the solar plexus, pancreas and liver)

Fourth chakra *Anahata* near the heart (associated with the cardiac plexus and thymus gland)

Fifth chakra *Visuddha* near the Adam's Apple in the throat (associated with the pharyngeal plexus and thyroid gland)

Sixth chakra *Ajna* between the eyebrows (associated with naso-ciliary plexus and pituitary gland)

Seventh chakra *Sahasrara* on the crown of the head (associated with the cerebrum and pineal gland)

As with any metaphysical system, it is important not to take the symbolism and metaphorical imagery too literally. Kundalini Yoga, after all, describes transformations of consciousness and is very much a process of exploring the 'inner reality' rather than representing a tangible, quantifiable endeavour. We find on examining the literature that there is also a certain amount of disparity — in the structure of the lotus *chakras*, in the colour symbolism of the Tattvas and even in perceptions of the experience itself. For example, Mahav Pandit ascribes a ten-petalled lotus to the heart *chakra, Anahata*, while Heinrich Zimmer and Swami Sivananda Radha describe it as twelve-petalled. Some writers represent the Tattva for *Akasha* as a black egg, others as a white circle, while the Tattva for *Svadisthana* is given by some as a silver crescent and by others as a white one.

In terms of experiencing the arousal of Kundalini itself — something which Tantric scholar and swami Agehananda Bharati describes as a basically 'imaginary' rather than physical process[15] there is also a certain amount of variance. According to Mircea Eliade, author of the classic work *Yoga: Immortality and Freedom*, the authentic arousal of Kundalini through all the *chakras* of the body is not only difficult but 'according to the Tantric authors themselves . . . rarely successful'[16] — usually because the breath cannot be restricted long enough to allow the *Shakti*-energy to rise the full length of *Sushumna*. However, according to Eliade, when it does occur the authentic release of Kundalini invariably generates intense heat and the lower part of the body becomes correspondingly inert and cold.

This is confirmed by Gopi Krishna, the yogi from Jammu in northern India, who aroused his Kundalini unexpectedly and experienced searing heat within his body — to such a dramatic extent that he feared he would die. Indeed, Gopi Krishna's unleashing of the Kundalini energy proved to be unbalanced and required a further visualisation to negate the heat. Suspecting that he had raised the energy not through the *Sushumna*, but through the hot, solar channel *Pingala*, he subsequently visualised the arousal of Kundalini through the cool, lunar channel *Ida*, and was able to counteract the 'devouring fire within'. Krishna's own account thus highlights the value of visualisation and lends credence to Bharati's view that the arousal of Kundalini is, in essence, imaginal rather than biophysical:

'With my mind reeling and senses deadened with pain, but with all the will-power left at my command, I brought my attention to bear on the left side of the seat of Kundalini, and tried to force an imaginary cold current upward through the middle of the spinal cord. In that extraordinary extended, agonised, and exhausted state of consciousness, I distinctly felt the location of the nerve and strained hard mentally to divert its flow into the central channel. Then, as if waiting for the destined moment, a miracle happened.

'There was a sound like a nerve thread snapping and instantaneously a silvery streak passed zig-zag through the spinal cord, exactly like the sinuous movement of a white serpent in rapid flight, pouring an effulgent, cascading shower of brilliant vital energy into my brain, filling my head with a blissful lustre in place of the flame that had been tormenting me for the last three hours. Completely taken by surprise at this sudden transformation of the fiery current, darting across the entire network of my nerves only a moment before, and overjoyed at the cessation of pain, I remained absolutely quiet and motionless for some time, tasting the bliss of relief with a mind flooded with emotion, unable to believe that I was really free of the horror. Tortured and exhausted almost to the point of collapse by the agony I had suffered during the terrible interval, I immediately fell asleep, bathed in light and for the first time after weeks of anguish felt the sweet embrace of restful sleep'.[17]

While accounts like Gopi Krishna's confirm the subjective nature of the Kundalini, that is not to deny its 'reality', for, as we have seen, the power of the imagination, and its importance in maintaining psychic balance can hardly be overstated. However Gopi Krishna's case does emphasise the need to treat metaphysical systems as symbolic frameworks and not get caught up in taking them too literally. This also enables us to compare related consciousness-expanding techniques as *parallel processes* without being distracted by their differences. For example there is a clear resemblance between the Middle Pillar of the Kabbalah and the *Sushumna* in Kundalini Yoga although the position of the *chakras (sephiroth)* varies, as do the colours and mantric names. The key point to remember is that in both systems the practitioner is engaging in an essentially mythic process of arousing internal energies and vibrations which have been personified as gods and goddesses. And, as the following summary shows, each *chakra* on the *Sushumna* has an accompanying range of symbolic ascriptions, including specific deities and 'seed mantras'. In addition the aim of arousing Kundalini is invariably described by the Tantric devotees themselves as an act of restoring the union of Shakti and Shiva — thereby emphasising the mythic or 'cosmic' nature of the Kundalini experience rather than its physiological aspects.

	Element	*Seed Mantra*	*God*	*Goddess*
Muladhara	Earth	'Lam'	Child Brahma	Dakini
Svadisthana	Water	'Vam'	Vishnu	Shakti Rakini
Manipura	Fire	'Ram'	Rudra	Lakini
Anahata	Air	'Yam'	Isa (Isvara)	Kakini
Visuddha	Spirit	'Ham'	Sadashiva	Gauri
Ajna	—	'Om'	Androgynous combination of Shakti and Shiva	
Sahasrara	—		— Total One-ness with Brahman —	

THE INDIVIDUAL CHAKRAS

Muladhara

The name of this chakra means 'root base' and it is both the foundation for personal growth and the gateway to the higher, 'more subtle' spheres. Jung identifies *Muladhara* with man's 'total consciousness of all outer and inner personal experiences' — not simply the physical world but our total awareness of everyday reality.[18]

The *chakra* consists of a crimson lotus with four petals, and includes within it the Tattva *Prithevi* — the yellow square of Earth. Within the yellow square is an inverted red triangle — a *yoni*, symbolic of Shakti herself. Within the triangle is a *linga*, and the serpent Kundalini lies coiled 3½ times around it, ready to be awakened. Below the triangle, but within the yellow square is a white seven-trunked elephant Airavata, which represents strength and sexual drive.

The deities ascribed to *Muladhara* are the Child Brahma and Dakini. Child Brahma has four arms and five faces and holds a staff (symbolising the human spine), a gourd (to quench thirst), and a rosary or *mala* (with 108 beads, representing the 108 names of Shakti). With his lower right hand he makes the gesture of dispelling fear.

Dakini has a single head and four arms. She holds a spear (purpose, resolve), a staff with a skull at one end (open to new ideas), a sword (discrimination) and a cup (the waters of Life).

Muladhara is associated with the sense of smell.

Svadisthana

Literally Shakti's 'own abode', *Svadhisthana* is the Kundalini Yoga counterpart of the Jungian 'unconscious' and the occult 'astral plane'. Regarded as the centre of the basic sexual instincts and desires, and a source of vital energy, it is appropriately associated with the genitals.

The *chakra* consists of a vermilion lotus with six petals and includes within it the Tattva *Apas* — the white crescent of Water — and also a smaller, eight-petalled lotus. Superimposed upon the crescent is a white water monster named Makara — a mythic blend of fish and crocodile. Jung compares this creature to the 'huge Leviathan which threatens us with annihilation'. According to Jung, entry into the unconscious is at first perceived as perilous, and rites of baptism are initiations which, through the element Water, confer purity. 'The way out of our *Muladhara* existence,' says Jung, 'leads into the water . . . One can approach the unconscious only in one way, namely by a purified mind, by the right attitude, and by the grace of heaven, which is the Kundalini'.[19]

The deities ascribed to *Svadisthana* are Vishnu and Shakti Rakini. Vishnu has four arms and holds a conch shell (for hearing the silence), a disc (symbolic of the mind), a club (to 'kill' the ego) and a lotus (symbol of purity and the sacred inner quest).

Shakti Rakini has four arms and holds a trident (three-fold division of body, mind and speech — Shakti being the Goddess of Speech), a lotus (purity), a drum (arousal) and a battle-axe (to overcome the obstacles of life).

Svadisthana is associated with the sense of taste.

Manipura

This *chakra* is known as 'the city (*pura*) of the lustrous gem (*mani*)' because of its association with the element Fire. Regarded as the primal source of high ambition, and associated with the will intent on obtaining power, it completes the triad of *chakras* (the other two being *Svadisthana* and *Muladhara*) which govern the lives of most people in their everyday environment. Jung notes that *Manipura* also represents the 'first light' of the rising sun which comes after baptism — the first real perception of the divinity within each human being. But he too identifies the *chakra* with ambition:

'A man who is not on fire is nothing . . . he is two-dimensional'.[20]

The *chakra* consists of a blue-black lotus with ten petals and includes within it the Tattva *Tejas* — the inverted red triangle of Fire. Leaping across the lower point of the triangle is a ram, which characterises the emotional obstructions to higher vision.

The deities ascribed to *Manipura* are Rudra and Lakini. Rudra, a form of Vishnu, has four arms and holds a rosary and fire weapon in his upper hands. With his lower ones he makes the gestures (*mudras*) of dispelling fear and granting favours.

Lakini has four arms and three faces, each with a third eye — indicating higher, spiritual perception. She holds a thunderbolt (power in Nature) and a fire weapon and, like Rudra, makes the gestures of dispelling fear and granting favours.

Manipura is associated with the sense of sight.

Anahata

Regarded as the centre of unselfish love and spiritual values, *Anahata* is the heart centre and the *chakra* most clearly associated with devotional mysticism. *Anahata* means 'unstruck sound' and it is in this *chakra* that god reaches down to touch his devotee who, for the first time, hears the sound (*sabda*) of Brahman.

Man has to overcome his emotions and the wind, or breath of life, lifts him up. The *chakra* is thus appropriately associated with the element Air: it consists of a vermilion lotus with twelve petals and includes within it the Tattva *Vayu* — a smoky grey hexagram.

At the lowest point of the hexagram is a black antelope — an animal known for its fleeting characteristics. It is an appropriate symbol for, as Swami Sivananda Radha writes, it represents 'spiritual experiences which go before the self can grasp them and know them'.[21] Nevertheless, the energies of this *chakra* call man on the spiritual quest, so that he can express higher values in his life.

The deities ascribed to *Anahata* are Isa (or Isvara) and Kakini. Isa has two arms and makes the gestures of dispelling fear and granting favours. Kakini has four arms: her upper hands hold a noose (symbolic of the act of being trapped into expecting spiritual experiences) and a staff with a skull (pure, open mind). Her lower hands make the gestures of dispelling fear and granting favours.

Anahata is associated with the sense of touch.

Visuddha

From the Sanskrit meaning 'completely purified', this *chakra* represents transcendence of the four basic elements and the encounter with Spirit. At the same time the devotee recognises that each individual life is a unique source of creative energy in the universe. Jung describes this centre as the *chakra* where the inner world is perceived to be more real than the physical. The act of arousing Kundalini, he notes, is essentially about 'the transformation of gross matter into the subtle matter of the mind . . . *Visuddha* is the world of abstract ideas and values, the world where the psyche exists in itself, where the psychical reality is the only reality, or where matter is only a thin skin around an enormous cosmos of psychical realities . . .'[22]

The *chakra* consists of a smoky-purple lotus with sixteen petals. Within it is an inverted white triangle (the *yoni* of Shakti) containing the Tattva *Akasha* — the white circle of Spirit. Within the circle is a very much diminished form of the white elephant Airavata, which is also found in *Muladhara*. However, whereas before it was a dominant force, it has now surrendered its strength in the service of the Spirit.

The deities ascribed to *Visuddha* are Sadashiva and Gauri. Sadashiva has five faces, each with three eyes — the third representing higher spiritual perception. A snake entwines his body indicating omniscience through the five senses. He has ten arms and holds a noose (a warning against pride), a goad (further 'pushing' is still required), a seven-headed snake (wisdom), a trident (body, mind, spirit), a fire symbol (ambition), a bell (attention), a diamond sceptre (power), a sword (the faculty of discrimination) and a battle-axe (to overcome the obstacles of the personality). With his remaining hand he makes the gesture of dispelling fear.

Gauri is the other half of Sadashiva's body. She has five faces and four arms, two of which similarly hold a goad and a noose. She also holds an arrow (clear direction) and a bow (tension, alertness).

Visuddha is associated with the sense of hearing.

Ajna and Sahasrara

The two remaining *chakras* represent transcendental states and are essentially beyond the scope of visualisation and the creative imagination. *Ajna* is known as the wisdom centre and is associated with the mystical experience called 'cosmic consciousness' in the West. In *Ajna* the complementary *nadis, Ida* and *Pingala*, join in a *chakra* for the first time since emerging from *Muladhara*. The mantra is OM and the ruling deity is androgynous — a combination of Shiva and Shakti in one form. In *Ajna* the consciousness of the yogi floods with divine radiance: he has become a *siddha*.

Sahasrara, the Lotus of a Thousand Petals, transcends duality altogether. Ruled by Paramashiva (the Supreme Shiva) this *chakra* is the doorway to the Void (*Sunya*). Here the union of Shakti and Shiva dissolves all manifested forms and there is only One-ness: Brahman.

Arousing Kundalini

The key factors in awakening Kundalini include controlled breathing (*pranayama*) and the use of seed mantras. In Kundalini Yoga the science of breathing is highly developed and it is advisable for the meditator to practise a variety of exercises, including breathing through alternate nostrils. However the key to arousing Kundalini is to retain the breath and focus on energising the *Muladhara* internally. Broad guidelines to this process — which is regarded still as 'secret' by many — are provided by Madhav Pandit in his book *Kundalini Yoga*, itself a condensation of Sir John Woodroffe's *The Serpent Power*:

'The sadhaka *sits in a prescribed asana and steadies the mind by concentrating between the eyebrows. Air is inhaled and retained; the upper part of the body is contracted and the* prana *(upward breath) is checked. The air thus prevented from going upward tends to rush downward; this escape of* vayu *as* apana *(downward breath) is also checked by appropriate contraction of the lower parts. The* vayu *thus collected is directed towards the* Muladhara *centre and the mind and will are concentrated upon it with the result that due to the frictional pressure of Prana and Apana held tight together, intense heat is generated and this again arouses the sleeping serpent Kundalini, which when so activated is drawn upwards. By mental concentration with the aid of mantra, the* jivatma *which is of the shape of a flame is brought down from the heart to the* Muladhara *and, so to say, united and moved along with the awakened Shakti. As its coils are loosened, the aperture to the door of Brahman,* Brahmadvara *at the mouth of the* Sushumna, *is opened and through the Citrini Nadi within, the Kundalini is led upwards'.*[23]

There is however a variant technique which is not included in Pandit's description and that relates to the energy of sexual orgasm. Kundalini Yoga is, after all, a form of Tantra and it is through the union of Shakti and Shiva that the bliss of *Samadhi* is obtained. The clues are provided in the *Muladhara chakra*, where the *linga* and the coiled serpent are depicted within the red *yoni* triangle of Shakti. I have it on good authority from an initiated Tantric yogi of the Bihar School of Yoga that the Kundalini can be unleashed by visualising a sexual interaction occurring within the *base* chakra. The male practitioner makes love to Shakti with his *linga* while a female devotee identifies Shakti's *yoni* with her own and visualises the *linga* entering in an act of sacred love-making. At the point of orgasm the energy released makes its way into the *Brahmadvara* and enters the *Sushumna*.

Each of the *chakras* has a seed mantra which is intoned in arousing the Kundalini from one level to the next. As each Tattva is visualised within its lotus, the seed mantra is intoned through it to activate it. Then, as the meditator 'lifts' the energy he imagines the mantra dissolving into the next Tattva above. For example, the *Muladhara chakra* is activated with the seed mantra 'Lam' and as the Kundalini rises towards *Svadisthana* this vibration is subsumed within the visualised water Tattva. The white crescent symbol is then activated by the seed mantra 'Vam' which in turn is dissolved into the fire Tattva. This sequence continues until *Visuddha* is reached, and at this point the seed mantra 'Ham' is dissolved into the body of Kundalini Shakti herself.

Note: In the East, the arousal of Kundalini is generally attended by a guru. As evidenced by the case of Gopi Krishna, intense psychic energies may be unleashed in the *Sushumna*, and if these energies flow into the wrong channel or prove too powerful, the experience can be both disturbing and painful. For this reason meditators should proceed with great care and work at a level that feels comfortable.

Having said that it is also true that the arousal of Kundalini can be profound and awesome: once one has had a peak experience — even involving the middle *chakras* — life literally takes on a new quality and meaning.

Perhaps the best advice that can be given — advice which is endorsed by mystical teachers universally — is to be pure in intent and proceed with humility, surrendering the limitations of the ego to the potentially infinite vision of the Higher Self.

WORKSHOP

KUNDALINI YOGA

TATTVA VISUALISATIONS FOR THE CHAKRAS

The following exercise should be practised for each of the chakra tattvas in turn, from Muladhara to Visuddha. Initially, you may like to practise one tattva each day, for 10-20 minutes.

Sit in a relaxed position, ideally in a full lotus asana or in a chair if that is more comfortable, and breathe deeply. Close your eyes and visualise the following tattvas, one at a time, persisting until you can hold the image clearly in your mind's eye:

Muladhara   a yellow square containing an inverted red triangle

Svadisthana   a white horizontal crescent (points upward)

Manipura   an inverted red triangle

Anahata   a smoky grey hexagram

Visuddha   a white circle

When you can visualise each of the tattvas clearly, practise vibrating the seed syllable through each tattva using each as a 'bridge' from one tattva to the next. The sequence is as follows:

Visualise the Muladhara tattva . . . intone *Lam*
Dissolve the *Lam* intonation as you begin to visualise the Svadisthana tattva.

Visualise the Svadisthana tattva . . . intone *Vam*
Dissolve the *Vam* intonation as you begin to visualise the Manipura tattva.

Visualise the Manipura tattva . . . intone *Ram*
Dissolve the *Ram* intonation as you begin to visualise the Anahata tattva.

Visualise the Anahata tattva . . . intone *Yam*
Dissolve the *Yam* intonation as you begin to visualise the Visuddha tattva.

Visualise the Visuddha tattva . . . intone *Ham*
Dissolve the *Ham* intonation into your own visualisation of Kundalini Shakti — the serpent energy.

Once this alteration of symbol and mantra has begun to work for you as a sequence, practise the same sequence but visualise the Kundalini energy rising through the chakras in their appropriate position on the body:

Muladhara   base of the spine

Svadisthana   just below the navel

Manipura   just above the navel

Anahata   near the heart

Visuddha   near the Adam's Apple in the throat

Since the Kundalini Shakti is traditionally associated with 'serpent fire' the arousal of Kundalini is appropriately linked to fire-music. Your selected music should be powerful and intense, suggestive of a current of life-force rising through the body!

Appropriate music: 'Dance 2' from Laraaji *Day of Radiance*

FOOTNOTES

CHAPTER ONE: MUSIC AND ALTERED STATES OF CONSCIOUSNESS

1 For an account of the two hemispheres of the brain see Robert E. Ornstein, *The Psychology of Consciousness* (1975)

2 This is a view advocated by psychoanalyst George Devereaux among others. See I.M. Lewis, *Ecstatic Religion* (1971) p. 180

3 The Menninger Institute in Kansas has conducted extensive research in this area. See Elmer and Alyce Green, *Beyond Biofeedback* (1977)

4 Erika Bourguignon, 'Altered States of Consciousness, Myths and Rituals' in B.M. Du Toit (ed.) *Drugs, Rituals and Altered States of Consciousness* (1977) p. 7

5 C.M. Bowra, *Primitive Song* (1962) p. 227

6 Weston La Barre, *The Ghost Dance* (1972) p. 421

7 Manfred Clynes (ed.) *Music, Mind and Brain* (1982) p. 174

8 A.J. Langguth, *Macumba* (1975) p. 70

9 Gregory Johnson, 'Hare Krishna in San Francisco' (1976) pp. 31-33

10 Bhagwan Shree Rajneesh, *The Orange Book* (1980), p. 31

11 Bhagwan Shree Rajneesh, *Get Out of your Own Way* (1977) p. 170

12 E.A. Wallis Budge, *The Bandlet of Righteousness* (1929) p. 3

13 Maurice Bouisson, *Magic: its Rites and History* (1960) p. 106

14 Mircea Eliade *Australian Religions* (1973) p. 135

15 E.A. Wallis Budge, *The Egyptian Book of the Dead* (1960) p. 4

16 Marius Schneider, *Primitive Music*, in E. Wellesz, *Ancient and Oriental Music* (1957) p. 43

17 Ibid. p. 49

18 Joan Halifax (ed.) *Shamanic Voices* (1979) p. 30

19 Ibid. p. 185

20 Castaneda's most vocal critic is psychologist Richard de Mille who has compiled an anthology of hostile articles under the titles *The Don Juan Papers* (1980). See also *Castaneda's Journey* (1976)

21 Michael Harner, *The Way of the Shaman* (1980) p. 3

22 Quoted in T.K. Oesterreich, *Possession: Demoniacal and Other* (1966) p. 336

23 Ibid. p. 340

24 Dane Rudyar, *The Magic of Tone and the Art of Music* (1982) p. 36

25 Unlike the Orphics, as John Pollard notes in his important book *Seers, Shrines and Sirens* (1965), the Pythagoreans 'practised asceticism . . . in order to increase the soul's awareness of the underlying principles which governed the universe. These were, of course, mathematical, and as such based more firmly on intellect than emotion'. (p. 114)

26 Lama Govinda, *Foundations of Tibetan Buddhism* (1967) p. 22

27 Agehananda Bharati, *The Tantric Tradition* (1965) p. 104

28 Lama Govinda, op cit. p. 22

29 Ibid. p. 23

30 Ibid. p. 23

31 Heinrich Zimmer, *Myths and Symbols in Indian Art and Civilization* (1962) p. 154

32 Lama Govinda, op cit. p. 47

33 Agehananda Bharati, op cit. p. 103

34 Robert Erickson, *Sound Structure in Music* (1975) p. 98

35 D. Polaczek, music critic for *Suddeutsche Zeitung*, quoted in Peter Michael Hamel, *Through Music to the Self* (1978), p. 74.

CHAPTER TWO: IMAGE AND ARCHETYPE

1 Carl E. Seashore, *Psychology of Music* (1967) p. 6

2 R. Wagner, *My Life* (1911) p. 314

3 F.R. Ritter, *Music and Musicians* (n.d.) p. 60

4 H. Berlioz, *The Life of Hector Berlioz* (1923) p. 232

5 Jerome Singer, *Daydreaming* (1966)

6 Sigmund Freud, *Standard Edition* (1953-66)

7 Angel Garma, *The Psychoanalysis of Dreams* (1967) p. 213

8 C.G. Jung, *Man and his Symbols* (1968) p. 12

9 Ibid. pp. 41-42

10 C.G. Jung, *Two Essays on Analytical Psychology* (1953) p. 68

11 Ibid. p. 70

12 Extract from a letter written by Carl Jung to a patient. See Gerhard Adler and Aniela Jaffe (eds) *Selected Letters of C.G. Jung*, Princeton University Press, 1973, pp. 459-60

13 Barbara Hannah, *Encounters with the Soul* (1981) p. 16

14 Ibid. p. 21

15 Mary Watkins, *Waking Dreams* (1976) p. 44

16 C.G. Jung, *Psychological Types* (1959) p. 78

17 C.G. Jung, *Civilisation in Transition* (1959) p. 769

18 John R. Battista, 'Images of Individuation' (1980) p. 119

19 James Hillman, *The Myth of Analysis* (1978) p. 155

20 James Hillman, *Revisioning Psychology* (1975) p. 30

21 Robert Avens, *Imagination is Reality* (1980) p. 93

22 James Hillman, *Psychology: Monotheistic or Polytheistic?* (1971) p. 298

23 David L. Miller, *The New Polytheism* (1974) pp. 6-7

24 Ibid. p. 55

25 Ibid. p. 56

26 James Hillman, *Revisioning Psychology* (1975) p. 207

27 Quoted in Robert Avens, *Imagination is Reality* (1980) p. 76

28 Ibid. p. 76

29 Wolfgang Kretschmer, 'Meditative Techniques in Psychotherapy' (1969) p. 224

30 Mary Watkins, *Waking Dreams* (1976) p. 109

31 Ibid. p. 61

32 David Levin, 'Approaches to Psychotherapy: Freud, Jung and Tibetan Buddhism' (1981) p. 262

33 Michael L. Emmons, 'The Inner Source and Meditative Therapy' (1980) p. 322

34 Dennis T. Jaffe and David E. Bresler, 'Guided Imagery: Healing through the Mind's Eye' (1980) pp. 253-54

35 Ibid. p. 260

36 Francis King (ed.) *Astral Projection, Ritual Magic and Alchemy* (1971) pp. 33-37

37 See also Francis King and Stephen Skinner, *Techniques of High Magic* (1976) pp. 54-59

38 Soror Vestigia's account is recorded in Israel Regardie, *The Golden Dawn* (Vol. 4 1940) p. 43

39 Ibid. p. 45

CHAPTER THREE: MUSIC FOR INNER SPACE

1 Carlos Castaneda, *Journey to Ixtlan* (1972)

2 John Lilly, *Simulations of God* (1975) pp. 146-47

3 Nevill Drury, *Inner Visions* (1979) pp. 36-37

4 See Mary Priestley, *Music Therapy in Action* (1975) pp. 251-58

5 Stanislav Grof, *LSD Psychotherapy* (1980) p. 155

6 Carl E. Seashore, *Psychology of Music* (1967) p. 6

7 For an account of this period see Art Kleps, *Millbrook* (1977) and also Timothy Leary, *Flashbacks* (1983)

8 From the sleeve notes: *Ambient One: Music for Airports*

9 From the sleeve notes: *Apollo*

10 Jim Aikin 'Steven Halpern — musical guru and new age entrepreneur' (1981) p. 8

11 Peter Michael Hamel, *Through Music to the Self* (1978) p. 100

CHAPTER FOUR: SELF-INITIATION

1 For the key passages of the *Greater Hekhaloth* see Aryeh Kaplan, *Meditation and Kabbalah* (1982)

2 Perle Epstein, *Kabbalah* (1979) p. 95

3 Francis King (ed.) *Astral Projection, Ritual Magic and Alchemy* (1971) p. 66

4 This text is from my now out-of-print book *Don Juan, Mescalito and Modern Magic* (1978)

5 Gareth Knight, *A Practical Guide to Qabalistic Symbolism* (1965) Vol. 2, p. 115

6 Hugh Lloyd-Jones, *Myths of the Zodiac* (1978) p. 94

7 Derek and Julia Parker, *A History of Astrology* (1983) p. 44

8 These are comparatively modern ascriptions since the planets Uranus and Neptune were not known in ancient times. Uranus was discovered in 1781 and Neptune in 1846

9 E.A. Wallis Budge, *The Egyptian Heaven and Hell* (1925) p. vii

10 Quoted in Adolf Erman, *A Handbook of Egyptian Religion* (1907) pp. 88-89

11 Ibid. p. 89

12 E.A. Wallis Budge, op cit. p. xii

13 Swami Sivananda Radha, *Kundalini Yoga for the West* (1981) p. 25 et seq.

14 C.G. Jung, *Psychological Commentary on Kundalini Yoga* (given on 26 October 1932) Published in *Spring* (1976) p. 17

15 It would perhaps have been more accurate to use the word 'imaginal' rather than 'imaginary' since the raising of the Kundalini obviously has its own experiential 'reality'. See Agehananda Bharati, *Light at the Center* (1976) p. 164

16 Mircea Eliade, *Yoga: Immortality and Freedom* (1969) p. 247

17 Gopi Krishna, *Kundalini* (1971) p. 66

18 C.G. Jung, *Psychological Commentary on Kundalini Yoga* (given on 12 October 1932) Published in *Spring* (1975) p. 9

19 Ibid. p. 10

20 Ibid. p. 26 (lecture given on 19 October 1932)

21 Swami Sivananda Radha, op cit. p. 163

22 C.G. Jung, *Psychological Commentary on Kundalini Yoga* (given on 26 October 1932) Published in *Spring* (1976) p. 6

23 M.P. Pandit, *Kundalini Yoga* (1968) pp. 54-55

BIBLIOGRAPHY

Aikin, J.,	'Steven Halpern — musical guru and new age entrepreneur', in *Keyboard* (USA) November, 1981
Ashcroft-Nowicki, D.,	*The Shining Paths*, Aquarian Press, Wellingborough, 1983
Assagioli, R.,	*Psychosynthesis*, Turnstone, London, 1975
Avens, R.,	*Imagination is Reality*, Spring Publications, Irving, Texas, 1980
Bardon, F.,	*The Practice of Magical Evocation*, Rudolf Pravica, Graz, 1967
Battista, J.R.,	'Images of Individuation' in Joseph E. Shorr et al. *Imagery*, Plenum, New York, 1980
Berlioz, H.,	*The Life of Hector Berlioz*, translated by Katherine F. Boult, Dutton, New York, 1923
Bharati, A.,	*The Light at the Center*, Ross Erikson, Santa Barbara, 1976 *The Tantric Tradition*, Rider, London, 1965
Bouisson, M.,	*Magic: its Rites and History*, Rider, London, 1960
Bourguignon, E.,	'Trance Dance', in John White (ed.)*The Highest State off Consciousness*, Doubleday, New York, 1972 'Altered States of Consciousness, Myths and Rituals, in B.M. Du Toit (ed.) *Drugs, Rituals and Altered States of Consciousness*, Balkema, Rotterdam, 1977 *Possession*, Chandler & Sharp, San Francisco, 1976
Bowra, C.M.,	*Primitive Song*, Weidenfeld & Nicholson, London, 1962
Budge, E.A.W.,	*The Bandlet of Righteousness*, Luzac, London, 1929 *The Egyptian Book of the Dead*, Routledge & Kegan Paul, London, 1960 *The Egyptian Heaven and Hell*, Martin Hopkinson, London, 1925
Campbell,	*The Hero with a Thousand Faces*, Princeton University Press, Princeton, 1968 *Myths to Live By*, Souvenir Press, London, 1973
Case, P.F.,	*The Tarot*, Macoy, New York, 1948
Castaneda, C.,	*Journey to Ixtlan*, Simon and Schuster, New York, 1971

Cavendish, R.,   *The Black Arts*, Routledge & Kegan Paul, London, 1967

Chaudhuri, H.,   'Yoga Psychology' in Charles Tart (ed.) *Transpersonal Psychologies*, Harper & Row, New York, 1975

Clynes, M.,   (ed.) *Music, Mind and Brain*, Plenum, New York, 1982

Colquhuon, I.,   *Sword of Wisdom*, Spearman, London, 1975

Court de Gebelin, A.,   *Le Monde Primitif*, Paris 1775-84 (nine Vols.)

Crowley, A.,   *Magic in Theory and Practice*, Routledge & Kegan Paul, London, 1973
   The Book of Thoth, Weiser, New York, 1969
   The Vision and the Voice, Sangreal Foundation, Dallas, 1972

De Mille, R.,   *Castaneda's Journey*, Capra, Santa Barbara, 1976
   The Don Juan Papers, Ross-Erikson, Santa Barbara, 1980

Desoille, R.,   *The Directed Daydream* (translated by Frank Haronian), Institute of Psychosynthesis, New York, 1966

Devereux, G.,   'Normal and Abnormal' in J.B. Casagrande and T. Gladwin (eds.) *Some Uses of Anthropology*, Washington, 1956

Drury, N.,   *The Path of the Chameleon*, Spearman, London, 1973
   Don Juan, Mescalito and Modern Magic, Routledge & Kegan Paul, London, 1978
   Inner Visions, Routledge & Kegan Paul, London 1979
   The Shaman and the Magician, Routledge and Kegan Paul, London, 1982
   Vision-Quest, Prism Press, Dorchester, 1984

Du Toit, B.M., (ed.)   *Drugs, Rituals and Altered States of Consciousness*, Balkema, Rotterdam, 1977

Edinger, E.,   *Ego and Archetype*, Pelican, Baltimore, 1973

Eliade, M.,   *Yoga: Immortality and Freedom*, Princeton University Press, Princeton, 1969
   Shamanism, Princeton University Press, Princeton, 1972
   Australian Religions, Cornell University Press, Ithaca, 1973

Elkin, A.P.,   *Aboriginal Men of High Degree*, University of Queensland Press, Brisbane, 1977

Emmons, M.L.   'The Inner Source and Meditative Therapy' in Joseph E. Shorr, *Imagery*, Plenum, New York, 1980

Epstein, P.,   *Kabbalah*, Weiser, New York, 1979

Erickson, R.,   *Sound Structure in Music*, University of California Press, Berkeley, 1975

Erman, A.,   *A Handbook of Egyptian Religion*, Constable, London, 1907

Etteilla,   *Maniere de se Recreer avec le Jeu de Cartes Nommes Tarots*, Amsterdam, 1783

Evans-Wentz, W.Y. (trans.),   *The Tibetan Book of the Dead*, Oxford University Press, New York, 1960

Fineberg, J., 'Imagery and Self-healing in *Nature & Health* Vol 5., no. 5, Sydney, 1984

Fortune, D., *The Mystical Qabalah*, Benn, London, 1966

Freud, S., *The Standard Edition of the Complete Psychological Works*, Vols 4-5 Hogarth Press, London, 1953-66

Garma, A., *The Psychoanalysis of Dreams*, Pall Mall, London, 1966

Gleadow, R., *The Origin of the Zodiac*, Atheneum, New York, 1969

Govinda, L.A., *Foundations of Tibetan Buddhism*, Rider, London, 1967

Green, E., & A., *Beyond Biofeedback*, Delacorte, New York, 1977

Grof, S., *Realms of the Human Unconscious*, Dutton, New York, 1976
LSD Psychotherapy, Hunter House, Pomona, California, 1980

Halifax, J., *Shamanic Voices*, Dutton, New York, 1979
Shaman, Crossroad, New York, 1982

Halpern, S., *Tuning the Human Instrument*, Halpern Sounds, Belmont, California, 1978

Hamel, P.M., *Through Music to the Self*, Compton Press, Salisbury, 1978 (first published by Scherz Verlag, Berne, 1976)

Hannah, B., *Encounters with the Soul*, Sigo Press, Santa Monica, California, 1981

Happich, C., *Anleitung zur Meditation*, E. Rother, Darmstadt, 1948

Harner, M., *The Way of the Shaman*, Harper & Row, San Francisco, 1980

Hillman, J., *The Myth of Analysis*, Harper & Row, New York, 1978
Psychology: Monotheistic or Polytheistic?, Spring Publications, New York, 1971
Revisioning Psychology, Harper & Row, New York, 1975
The Dream and the Underworld, Harper & Row, New York, 1979

Howe, E., *The Magicians of the Golden Dawn*, Routledge & Kegan Paul, London, 1972

Huxley, A., *The Doors of Perception/Heaven and Hell*, Penguin, Harmondsworth, 1959

Jaffe, D.T., and Bresler, D.E., 'Guided Imagery: Healing through the Mind's Eye' in Joseph E. Shorr, *Imagery*, Plenum, New York, 1980

Johnson, G., 'Hare Krishna in San Francisco' in Charles Y. Glock and Robert N. Bellah (eds) *The New Religious Consciousness*, University of California Press, Berkeley, 1976

Johnston, W., *Silent Music*, Collins, London, 1974.

Jung, C.G., *Man and his Symbols*, Dell, New York, 1968
Two Essays on Analytical Psychology, Routledge & Kegan Paul, London, 1953
Civilisation in Transition, Routledge & Kegan Paul, London, 1959

Psychological Commentary on Kundalini (Lectures One and Two, and Lectures Three and Four)*Spring*, New York, 1975 and 1976 respectively
Psychological Types, Routledge & Kegan Paul, London, 1959

Kaplan, A., (ed.)   *The Bahir*, Weiser, New York, 1979
Meditation and Kabbalah, Weiser, York Beach, Maine, 1982

King, F., (ed.)   *Astral Projection, Ritual Magic and Alchemy*, Spearman, London, 1971

King, F., and   *Techniques of High Magic*, Daniel, London, 1976
Skinner, S.,

Kleps, A.,   *Millbrook*, Bench Press, Oakland, California, 1977

Knight, G.,   *A Practical Guide to Qabalistic Symbolism*, Helios, Cheltenham, 1965

Kretschmer, W.,   'Meditative Techniques in Psychotherapy' in Charles Tart (ed.) *Altered States of Consciousness*, Wiley, New York, 1969

Krishna, G.,   *Kundalini*, Robinson & Watkins, London, 1971

La Barre, W.,   *The Ghost Dance*, Allen & Unwin, London, 1972

Langguth, A.J.,   *Macumba*, Harper & Row, New York, 1975

Leary, T.,   *The Psychedelic Experience*, University Books, New York, 1964
High Priest, College Notes & Texts, New York, 1968
Flashbacks, Tarcher, Los Angeles, 1983

Leuner, H., and   'Initiated Symbol Projection', in Roberto Assagioli,
Kornadt, H.J.,   *Psychosynthesis*, Turnstone, London, 1975

Levin, D.,   'Approaches to Psychotherapy: Freud, Jung and Tibetan Buddhism' in Ronald S. Valle and Rolf von Eckartsberg (eds.) *The Metaphors of Consciousness*, Plenum, New York, 1981

Lewis, I.M.,   *Ecstatic Religion*, Penguin, Harmondsworth, 1971

Lilly, J.,   *Centre of the Cyclone*, Paladin, London, 1973
Simulations of God, Simon and Schuster, New York, 1975

Lloyd-Jones, H., *Myths of the Zodiac*, Duckworth, London, 1978

Masters, R., and *Mind Games*, Turnstone, London, 1973
Houston, J.,

Mathers, S.L.M., *The Kabbalah Unveiled*, Redway, London, 1887

Metzner, R.,   *Maps of Consciousness*, Macmillan, New York, 1971

Mumford, J.,   *Psychosomatic Yoga*, Aquarian, Wellingborough, 1979

Miller, D.,   *The New Polytheism*, Harper & Row, New York, 1974

Ornstein, R.E.,   *The Psychology of Consciousness*, Pelican, Baltimore, 1975
The Mind Field, Grossman/Viking, New York, 1976

Oesterreich, T.K., *Possession, Demoniacal and Other*, University Books, New York, 1966

Pandit, M.P., *Kundalini Yoga*, Ganesh, Madras, 1968

Papus, *The Tarot of the Bohemians*, Rider, London, 1919

Parker, D. and J., *A History of Astrology*, Deutsch, London, 1983

Pollard, J. *Seers, Shrines and Sirens*, Allen & Unwin, London, 1965

Priestley, M., *Music Therapy in Action*, Constable, London, 1975

Radha, S.S., *Kundalini Yoga for the West*, Shambhala, Boulder, Colorado, 1981

Rajneesh, B.S., *The Orange Book*, Rajneesh Foundation International Rajneeshpuram, Oregon, 1980
Get Out Of Your Own Way, Rajneesh Foundation International, Rajneeshpuram, Oregon, 1977

Regardie, I., *The Tree of Life*, Weiser, New York, 1968
The Golden Dawn, (Four vols.) Aries Press, Chicago, 1937-40. Republished various editions.

Ritter, F.R., *Music and Musicians*, Reeves, London (n.d.)

Rudyar, D., *The Magic of Tone and the Art of Music*, Shambhala, Boulder, Colorado, 1982

Samuels, M. & N., *Seeing with the Mind's Eye*, Random House, New York, 1975

Schaya, L., *The Universal Meaning of the Kabbalah*, University Books, New York, 1971

Schneider, M., 'Primitive Music' in E. Wellesz, *Ancient and Oriental Music*, Oxford University Press, 1957

Scholem, G., *Major Trends in Jewish Mysticism*, Schocken, New York, 1961

Seashore, C.E., *Psychology of Music*, Dover, New York, 1967

Shorr, J.E. et al. (eds) *Imagery*, Plenum, New York, 1980

Singer, J., *Daydreaming*, Random House, New York, 1966

Tart, C. (ed.) *Altered States of Consciousness*, Wiley, New York, 1969
Transpersonal Psychologies, Harper & Row, New York, 1975

Waite, A.E., *The Pictorial Key to the Tarot*, Weiser, New York, 1963

Wagner, R., *My Life*, Dodd Mead, New York, 1911

Watkins, M., *Waking Dreams*, Gordon & Breach, New York, 1976

White, J., (ed.) *The Highest State of Consciousness*, Doubleday, New York, 1972

Woodroffe, J., *The Serpent Power*, Ganesh, Madras, 1964

Yeats, W.B., *Mythologies*, Macmillan, London, 1959

Zimmer, H., *Myths and Symbols in Indian Art and Civilization*, Harper and Bros., New York, 1962

Zuckerkandl, V., *Man the Musician*, (Vol. 2) Princeton University Press, Princeton, 1973